# THE
# Essential Home
# Record Book

## READY-TO-USE FORMS
## FOR ALL YOUR PERSONAL,
## MEDICAL, HOUSEHOLD, AND
## FINANCIAL INFORMATION

### PAMELA K. PFEFFER

A PLUME BOOK

To my God and to my family
who love and encourage me.

PLUME
Published by the Penguin Group
Penguin Books USA Inc., 375 Hudson Street, New York, New York 10014, U.S.A.
Penguin Books Ltd, 27 Wrights Lane, London W8 5TZ, England
Penguin Books Australia Ltd, Ringwood, Victoria, Australia
Penguin Books Canada Ltd, 10 Alcorn Avenue, Toronto, Ontario, Canada M4V 3B2
Penguin Books (N.Z.) Ltd, 182–190 Wairau Road, Auckland 10, New Zealand

Penguin Books Ltd, Registered Offices:
Harmondsworth, Middlesex, England

First published by Plume, an imprint of Dutton Signet,
a division of Penguin Books USA Inc.

First Printing, March, 1997
 3  5  7  9  10  8  6  4

Ⓟ REGISTERED TRADEMARK—MARCA REGISTRADA

ISBN 0-452-27612-8

Printed in the United States of America
Set in Janson Text and Gill Sans
Designed by Jesse Cohen

# CONTENTS

## Insurance Records    *151*

# ACKNOWLEDGMENTS

Since this book began as a handout for a seminar, I must first thank Ruthie Brown Cook, the bank officer who organized the program. Without that event, I would have never written the pages that follow. Then, I want to thank my husband, Phil, our boys, John-Lindell and his wife, Maria, Jamie, and David. They have had to listen to me over and over talking to everyone—questioning, probing, writing. Even though I am sure there have been many times they were tired of the whole project, they remained sweet and encouraging. I must also thank my extended family. My sister Jan, as a financial advisor, had many insights. My parents, Jean and John Easley, and my in-laws, Phil and Jeanne Pfeffer, endured endless questions that helped me understand the thoughts and needs of their generation. Then I must thank so many friends, each of whom is an expert in his or her way as a doctor, dentist, lawyer, banker, friends with children who are younger than mine, car salesman, boat saleswoman, realtor . . . even those who were complete strangers who looked over my shoulder on airplanes and in hotel lobbies. An amazing number of people became interested and offered wonderful suggestions. Any project is enhanced by such insights, and I thank each and every one of them.

# WHO NEEDS THIS BOOK?

Who needs *The Essential Home Record Book*? YOU DO!

If you had a medical emergency, could you quickly find your health history and information about your insurance coverage? Do you have a record of your bank and credit card accounts in one convenient place? What are the birthdates and Social Security numbers of all your family members? Would your baby-sitter know who to contact in an emergency if you couldn't be reached? Do you have an itemized list of your valuable property? When did your pets last get their shots?

Chances are that this vital information is scattered in various places in your home or office, and out of easy reach to you or your family. Now, using the forms provided in this book, all of your important personal, financial, and medical data can be organized in a one-stop resource.

This book makes it easy for *anyone* to become organized. If you are already an organized person, you will love having all this information at your fingertips. If you are not even close to being organized, you'll be thankful for the many simple, fill-in-the-blank forms that can help even the most disorganized person stay on top of the critical information that you need for everyday reference and especially in an emergency.

I can just hear you saying, "Look at all those forms! I can't possibly be bothered filling all of them out."

My answer to that objection: *Do not even try to do it all at once.* And not everyone will need every page. Complete those that make sense for you. Start by filling in basic information about your family, your home, and your finances. Once you have recorded those details, add information every time you get a new credit card, open a new loan, or buy a new major appliance. It takes only a few minutes to update your records and can save you valuable time later.

Those who are already superorganized might object, "I already have that information in my files. I don't need this book."

But while *you* may know where everything is, does your spouse know where to find this information if you're not available? Do your children? By completing the records in this book, you'll provide them with the information they need to handle any emergency.

So, who needs this book? You do!

# HOW TO USE THESE FORMS

There are several ways you can work with this book to establish your family's important records.

## Write Directly in This Book

You may find it easiest simply to fill in the forms included in this book. That way you'll have in one handy place all the information you need to keep track of your records. For this reason, several copies of the same form are provided so you'll have enough room to list all of your accounts, properties, assets, etc. You might want to consider giving each family member their own copy for ready reference. And don't forget to send copies to children and in-laws who may live hundreds of miles away—if they're contacted in an emergency, knowing which doctor to call or what neighbor can pick up the kids may prove invaluable.

## Make Copies of the Forms in This Book

If you want to reuse these forms, you may prefer to make photocopies of the individual forms that you need and keep them together in your own loose-leaf file or pocket organizer. This way you can quickly and easily replace forms as the information becomes outdated. Just remember to keep the forms in approximately the same order they appear in this book. That way you'll have medical, financial, personal, etc., information together in one place. You may want to use tabbed dividers to help you organize.

## Use These Forms to Set Up Your Own Computer Records

If you're at home using a personal computer, you may want to store all of your information electronically. The forms included here will help you set up your files and highlight the information you'll want to include. Remember to organize the files in a convenient, timesaving way—i.e., set up individual files for financial records, medical information, personal data, etc. Also, be sure another family member knows the password and the names of the files in the event you can't be reached in an emergency.

Some other tips:

## Pick a Category

Don't try to complete the whole book at once. Begin by selecting a category and filling in the forms there first. Your most important category may be different from someone else's. For example, the Home or Family section may be the place to start for some people. Others may feel it's more important to complete the forms in the medical section first.

## Copy as You Go

While you will want to keep your important documents together in this book, your notebook, or on your computer, you may also want to keep additional copies stored in a safe deposit box or in another notebook kept in a different location. Make copies of completed forms as necessary.

## Record Information Promptly

After you have made a record of your basic vital information, your financial, medical, and personal status will continue to change. When you open a new bank account, record the pertinent information right away. When you buy that new computer or stereo, record its serial number on the day you get it. Get into the habit—enter *all* important information before you forget.

## The Value of a Checklist

The checklists in this book have been designed to help you know what information you have at a glance. As you complete a form, check it off in the space provided. This will allow you to track your progress and point out areas where information is needed.

# MASTER CHECKLIST OF FORMS

**In an Emergency**
☐ Emergency Numbers
☐ Emergency Identification

**Personal and Family Records**
☐ Family Summary
☐ Personal Background
☐ Adoption Information
☐ Summary of Personal Advisers
☐ Résumés
☐ Children's School Records
☐ Children's Schedules
☐ Baby-sitter's Log
☐ Where Parents Can Be Reached
☐ Family Birthdays
☐ Important Dates to Remember
☐ Volunteer and Community
    Commitments
☐ Other Names and Addresses
☐ Travel Itenerary
☐ Packing Checklist
☐ Clothing Sizes
☐ Pet Records
☐ Funeral and Burial Instructions
    ☐ Pallbearers
    ☐ To Be Notified in Case of Death
    ☐ Distribution of Property

**Your Home**
☐ Location of Important Documents
☐ Computer File Records

☐ Important Utility Locations
☐ Home Maintenance Log
☐ Personal Services
☐ Appliance Checklist
☐ Home Inspection Checklist
☐ Recycling Information
☐ Emergency Numbers at Vacation
    Home
☐ Home Inventory Records

**Medical Records**
☐ Doctors' Numbers
☐ Personal Medical History
☐ Medical Family Tree
☐ Consent Form for Emergency
    Medical Treatment and/or Surgery
    for a Minor
☐ Living Will

**Financial Records**
☐ Bank Accounts
☐ Credit Card Accounts
☐ Real Estate—Owned
☐ Real Estate—Leased
☐ Safe Deposit Box
☐ Stocks, Bonds, T-Bills, and Other
    Financial Assets
☐ Other Investments
☐ Other Assets (Antiques, Art,
    Jewelry, etc.)
☐ Vehicle Records—Owned

☐ Vehicle Records—Leased
☐ Boat Records
☐ Business Ownership Information
☐ Expense Report—Business
☐ Expense Report—Personal
☐ Charitable Contributions
☐ Business Gifts
☐ Receivables
☐ Liabilities (Non–Real Estate)
☐ Liabilities (Vehicle Lease)
☐ Trust Funds
☐ Retirement Income
    ☐ Social Security Benefits
    ☐ IRA/Keogh
    ☐ Annuities
    ☐ Pension Plans
☐ Durable Power-of-Attorney

**Insurance Records**
☐ Insurance Summary
☐ Disability Insurance
☐ Health/Dental/Major Medical
    Insurance
☐ Life Insurance
☐ Long-Term-Care Insurance
☐ Property Insurance
☐ Umbrella Insurance
☐ Vehicle/Boat Insurance
☐ Other Insurance

**Extended Family Records**
☐ Emergency Numbers
☐ Location of Important Documents
☐ Medical History
☐ Key Advisers and Contacts
☐ Distribution of Property
☐ Living Will
☐ Durable Power-of-Attorney

# IN AN EMERGENCY

# EMERGENCY NUMBERS

Home address: _____ Zip: _____

Home phone: _____, _____, _____

Mobile phone/Beeper: _____, _____, _____

Directions from nearest major intersection:

_____

_____

_____

_____

Fire Dept. #: _____ Police #: _____

Ambulance #: _____

Poison control #: _____ Home alarm company #: _____

Code #: _____

Hospital—Name: _____ Phone: _____

Address: _____

Mother's work #: _____ Father's work #: _____

Family doctor—Name: _____ Phone: _____

Pediatrician—Name: _____ Phone: _____

Pet emergency #: _____

Drugstore #: _____

Drugstore that delivers #: _____

Relative: _____ Relationship: _____

Address: _____

Home #: _____ Office #: _____ Mobile #: _____

Relative: _____ Relationship: _____

Address: _____

Home #: _____ Office #: _____ Mobile #: _____

Neighbor: _____

Address: _____

Home #: _____ Office #: _____ Mobile #: _____

Neighbor: _____

Address: _____

Home #: _____ Office #: _____ Mobile #: _____

# EMERGENCY IDENTIFICATION INFORMATION

**Keep this form up-to-date and pass out to friends, family, and authorities in an emergency.**

Full name: _____ Name called: _____

Address: _____

Phone: _____ Social Security number: _____

Date of birth: _____ Place of birth: _____

Sex: _____ Blood type: _____ Ethnic background: _____

Height: _____ Weight: _____ Eyes: _____ Hair: _____

Identifying features: _____

_____

Is a photograph available?: _____ Where?: _____

Emergency contacts

Name: _____ Relationship: _____

Address: _____ Phone: _____

Name: _____ Relationship: _____

Address: _____ Phone: _____

Name: _____ Relationship: _____

Address: _____ Phone: _____

Name: _____ Relationship: _____

Address: _____ Phone: _____

Doctor: _____ Phone: _____

Dentist (dental records): _____ Phone: _____

Local police/Missing-persons phone: _____

**Have local police fingerprint your family/children and attach.**

The National Center for Missing & Exploited Children 1-800-THE-LOST

# EMERGENCY IDENTIFICATION INFORMATION

**Keep this form up-to-date and pass out to friends, family, and authorities in an emergency.**

Full name: _____ Name called: _____

Address: _____

Phone: _____ Social Security number: _____

Date of birth: _____ Place of birth: _____

Sex: _____ Blood type: _____ Ethnic background: _____

Height: _____ Weight: _____ Eyes: _____ Hair: _____

Identifying features: _____

_____

Is a photograph available?: _____ Where?: _____

Emergency contacts

    Name: _____ Relationship: _____

      Address: _____ Phone: _____

    Name: _____ Relationship: _____

      Address: _____ Phone: _____

    Name: _____ Relationship: _____

      Address: _____ Phone: _____

    Name: _____ Relationship: _____

      Address: _____ Phone: _____

Doctor: _____ Phone: _____

Dentist (dental records): _____ Phone: _____

Local police/Missing-persons phone: _____

**Have local police fingerprint your family/children and attach.**

The National Center for Missing & Exploited Children 1-800-THE-LOST

# EMERGENCY IDENTIFICATION INFORMATION

**Keep this form up-to-date and pass out to friends, family, and authorities in an emergency.**

Full name: _____ Name called: _____

Address: _____

Phone: _____ Social Security number: _____

Date of birth: _____ Place of birth: _____

Sex: _____ Blood type: _____ Ethnic background: _____

Height: _____ Weight: _____ Eyes: _____ Hair: _____

Identifying features: _____

_____

Is a photograph available?: _____ Where?: _____

Emergency contacts

   Name: _____ Relationship: _____

     Address: _____ Phone: _____

   Name: _____ Relationship: _____

     Address: _____ Phone: _____

   Name: _____ Relationship: _____

     Address: _____ Phone: _____

   Name: _____ Relationship: _____

     Address: _____ Phone: _____

Doctor: _____ Phone: _____

Dentist (dental records): _____ Phone: _____

Local police/Missing-persons phone: _____

**Have local police fingerprint your family/children and attach.**

The National Center for Missing & Exploited Children 1-800-THE-LOST

# EMERGENCY IDENTIFICATION INFORMATION

Keep this form up-to-date and pass out to friends, family, and authorities in an emergency.

Full name: _____ Name called: _____

Address: _____

Phone: _____ Social Security number: _____

Date of birth: _____ Place of birth: _____

Sex: _____ Blood type: _____ Ethnic background: _____

Height: _____ Weight: _____ Eyes: _____ Hair: _____

Identifying features: _____

_____

Is a photograph available?: _____ Where?: _____

Emergency contacts

  Name: _____ Relationship: _____

  Address: _____ Phone: _____

  Name: _____ Relationship: _____

  Address: _____ Phone: _____

  Name: _____ Relationship: _____

  Address: _____ Phone: _____

  Name: _____ Relationship: _____

  Address: _____ Phone: _____

Doctor: _____ Phone: _____

Dentist (dental records): _____ Phone: _____

Local police/Missing-persons phone: _____

**Have local police fingerprint your family/children and attach.**
The National Center for Missing & Exploited Children 1-800-THE-LOST

Copyright © 1997 Pamela K. Pfeffer

# PERSONAL AND FAMILY RECORDS

This section begins with summaries of important information about your family—everything from birthdates to blood types. Hopefully, you will never be late for a birthday or anniversary again. There is even a form to help you remember clothing sizes for those who are important in your life. Then to assist you in keeping up with all of the other people and businesses in your life is a simple format for a database or Rolodex. I encourage you to start simple and build into a more complete format. If you are not convinced of the value of this information file, our good friend Harvey Mackay in his book *Swim With the Sharks* says it is his key to success. He has a database that is fine-tuned and incredible. When he visits, sometimes I think he knows more about us than we know about ourselves! Take a little time to get your basic address book entered into the database format. Add information as it becomes available. In no time at all you will wonder how you ever functioned without it!

Then there is information needed for children. This information is invaluable for a baby-sitter whether you are just out for dinner or out of town for a few days. I do recommend making copies as needed for baby-sitters so other information in this book can remain confidential. If you are out of town, you may need pass on to a baby-sitter and/or house sitter such things as emergency numbers, information on pets, and your travel itinerary.

For your travel convenience, and to make sure you have not forgotten anything, I have included a form for basic travel itinerary information and a checklist to assist you when packing. While the checklist looks as if the only thing not included is the kitchen sink, let me assure you that you can have all of this and still travel with only a carry-on suitcase. I do regularly. And these trips include ten-day business trips to Europe. There are some simple tricks to make it work. First, buy small travel-size containers. Second, when you are buying clothes, think about how well the item will pack. Third, coordinate, make a piece of clothing work in more than one way. Plan around one color scheme. Last, learn how to pack. For example, underwear can go in shoes, helping protect your shoes and not wasting the space. Then roll, roll, roll your clothes. For men with business suits and starched shirts, fold clothes over each other to prevent creasing. When you arrive, take the clothes out for the evening or the next day. If there are a few wrinkles, hang them in the bathroom and turn the shower on hot. Close the door and steam away those wrinkles.

Also included in this section on family is information on your personal background. This will be quick and easy to complete, and may someday be important. With so many people changing jobs these days, a current résumé is necessary. It will be far easier to keep it current if you review it annually than if you allow several years to go by without updating it. If any member of your family is adopted, some additional information may be helpful.

Hopefully, you will never need the page on emergency identification information. Unfortunately, kidnappings, runaways, disappearances of Alzheimer's victims, and so forth happen all too often. Be sure to update regularly. For children, I suggest updating annually. If you should ever need this page, it will be an enormous help to have it available and current.

Finally, there is a form on funeral and burial information. I urge you to complete this immediately while everyone is healthy and not under the stress of personal loss. Make sure you know what your loved ones want, and make sure they know what you want. When the need arises, this will make it far easier on the survivors.

# FAMILY SUMMARY

| Full Legal Name | Birth Date | Social Security # | Blood Type | Driver's License # |
| --- | --- | --- | --- | --- |
| _____ | _____ | _____ | _____ | _____ |
| _____ | _____ | _____ | _____ | _____ |
| _____ | _____ | _____ | _____ | _____ |
| _____ | _____ | _____ | _____ | _____ |
| _____ | _____ | _____ | _____ | _____ |
| _____ | _____ | _____ | _____ | _____ |
| _____ | _____ | _____ | _____ | _____ |
| _____ | _____ | _____ | _____ | _____ |
| _____ | _____ | _____ | _____ | _____ |
| _____ | _____ | _____ | _____ | _____ |
| _____ | _____ | _____ | _____ | _____ |
| _____ | _____ | _____ | _____ | _____ |
| _____ | _____ | _____ | _____ | _____ |
| _____ | _____ | _____ | _____ | _____ |
| _____ | _____ | _____ | _____ | _____ |
| _____ | _____ | _____ | _____ | _____ |
| _____ | _____ | _____ | _____ | _____ |
| _____ | _____ | _____ | _____ | _____ |
| _____ | _____ | _____ | _____ | _____ |

# PERSONAL BACKGROUND

Name: _____ Maiden: _____

Birth date: _____ Birthplace: _____

If citizen of foreign country, country: _____

Date entered U.S.: _____ Visa status: _____

Father's name: _____

Birth date: _____ Birthplace: _____

If deceased—Date: _____ Cause of death: _____

Mother's name: _____ Maiden: _____

Birth date: _____ Birthplace: _____

If deceased—Date: _____ Cause of death: _____

Marital status: Single _____ Married _____ Divorced _____ Widowed _____

If married—Date: _____ Location: _____

If widowed—Date: _____ Cause of death: _____

If divorced—Date: _____ Location: _____

Spouse: _____ Maiden: _____

Birth date: _____ Birthplace: _____

Former spouse: _____ Maiden: _____

Children:    <u>Name</u>            <u>Date of birth</u>    <u>Place of birth</u>

_____    _____    _____

_____    _____    _____

_____    _____    _____

Brothers and Sisters:    <u>Name</u>    <u>Date of birth</u>    <u>Place of birth</u>

_____    _____    _____

_____    _____    _____

_____    _____    _____

# PERSONAL BACKGROUND

Name: _____ Maiden: _____

Birth date: _____ Birthplace: _____

If citizen of foreign country, country: _____

Date entered U.S.: _____ Visa status: _____

Father's name: _____

Birth date: _____ Birthplace: _____

If deceased—Date: _____ Cause of death: _____

Mother's name: _____ Maiden: _____

Birth date: _____ Birthplace: _____

If deceased—Date: _____ Cause of death: _____

Marital status: Single _____ Married _____ Divorced _____ Widowed _____

If married—Date: _____ Location: _____

If widowed—Date: _____ Cause of death: _____

If divorced—Date: _____ Location: _____

Spouse: _____ Maiden: _____

Birth date: _____ Birthplace: _____

Former spouse: _____ Maiden: _____

Children:    Name                Date of birth    Place of birth

_____    _____    _____

_____    _____    _____

_____    _____    _____

Brothers and Sisters:    Name    Date of birth    Place of birth

_____    _____    _____

_____    _____    _____

_____    _____    _____

# ADOPTION INFORMATION

Name: _____

Adoption agency: _____

   Address: _____ Phone: _____

Lawyer: _____

   Address: _____ Phone: _____

Dates of surrender: _____ Petition: _____ Adoption: _____

Location of adoption city: _____ County: _____ State: _____

Location of documents: _____

**Background: Biological/Medical.** Complete as much as possible of a Medical Family Tree form (p. 91) for each known biological relative.

   Were there problems with delivery?: _____

      If yes, give known details: _____

   Did birth mother have prior miscarriages, stillbirths?: _____

      If yes, give known details: _____

|  | **Mother** | **Father** |
|---|---|---|
| Ethnic background: | _____ | _____ |
| Hair color: | _____ | _____ |
| Eye color: | _____ | _____ |
| Skin color: | _____ | _____ |
| Genetic problems:* | _____ | _____ |
|  | _____ | _____ |
| Other: | _____ | _____ |
|  | _____ | _____ |

*For example, carrier of cystic fibrosis gene, family susceptible to breast cancer, etc.

# ADOPTION INFORMATION

Name: _____

Adoption agency: _____

    Address: _____ Phone: _____

Lawyer: _____

    Address: _____ Phone: _____

Dates of surrender: _____ Petition: _____ Adoption: _____

Location of adoption city: _____ County: _____ State: _____

Location of documents: _____

**Background: Biological/Medical.** Complete as much as possible of a Medical Family Tree form (p. 91) for each known biological relative.

    Were there problems with delivery?: _____

      If yes, give known details: _____

    Did birth mother have prior miscarriages, stillbirths?: _____

      If yes, give known details: _____

| | **Mother** | **Father** |
|---|---|---|
| Ethnic background: | _____ | _____ |
| Hair color: | _____ | _____ |
| Eye color: | _____ | _____ |
| Skin color: | _____ | _____ |
| Genetic problems:* | _____ | _____ |
| | _____ | _____ |
| Other: | _____ | _____ |
| | _____ | _____ |

*For example, carrier of cystic fibrosis gene, family susceptible to breast cancer, etc.

Copyright © 1997 Pamela K. Pfeffer

# SUMMARY OF PERSONAL ADVISERS

Accountant: _____ Phone: _____

   Address: _____

Attorney: _____ Phone: _____

   Address: _____

Attorney: _____ Phone: _____

   Address: _____

Bank: _____ Branch: _____

Banker: _____ Phone: _____

   Address: _____

Bank: _____

Banker: _____ Phone: _____

   Address: _____

Church: _____

Clergy: _____ Phone: _____

   Address: _____

Financial Adviser: _____ Phone: _____

   Address: _____

Insurance Agent: _____

   Disability: _____ Phone: _____

      Address: _____

   Health: _____ Phone: _____

      Address: _____

   Life: _____ Phone: _____

      Address: _____

   Marine/Boat: _____ Phone: _____

      Address: _____

   Real Estate: _____ Phone: _____

      Address: _____

Vehicle: _____ Phone: _____

    Address: _____

Realtor: _____ Phone: _____

    Address: _____

Stockbroker company: _____

Stockbroker: _____ Phone: _____

    Address: _____

Stockbroker company: _____

Stockbroker: _____ Phone: _____

    Address: _____

Trust company: _____

Trust officer: _____ Phone: _____

    Address: _____

_____ Phone: _____

    Address: _____

_____ Phone: _____

    Address: _____

_____ Phone: _____

    Address: _____

_____ Phone: _____

    Address: _____

_____ Phone: _____

    Address: _____

_____ Phone: _____

    Address: _____

_____ Phone: _____

# RÉSUMÉ

Name: _____ SSN: _____

## Current Position

Company: _____ Phone: _____

Address: _____

Position(s): _____ Dates: _____

_____    _____

_____    _____

Description of responsibilities: _____

_____

_____

Contact name: _____ Phone: _____

Position: _____

## Previous Positions

Company: _____ Phone: _____

Address: _____

Position(s): _____ Dates: _____

_____    _____

_____    _____

Description of responsibilities: _____

_____

_____

Contact name: _____ Phone: _____

Position: _____

# RÉSUMÉ (CONTINUED)

Company: _____ Phone: _____

Address: _____

Position(s): _____ Dates: _____

_____ _____

_____ _____

Description of responsibilities: _____

_____

_____

Contact name: _____ Phone: _____

Position: _____

Company: _____ Phone: _____

Address: _____

Position(s): _____ Dates: _____

_____ _____

_____ _____

Description of responsibilities: _____

_____

_____

Contact name: _____ Phone: _____

Position: _____

# RÉSUMÉ (CONTINUED)

Company: _____ Phone: _____

Address: _____

Position(s): _____ Dates: _____

_____   _____

_____   _____

Description of responsibilities: _____

_____

_____

Contact name: _____ Phone: _____

Position: _____

## Community, religious, and volunteer involvement

| Name of Group | Work or position | Dates |
| --- | --- | --- |
| | | |
| | | |
| | | |
| | | |

## Special awards, recognitions, achievements: _____

_____

# RÉSUMÉ

Name: _____ SSN: _____

## Current Position

Company: _____ Phone: _____

Address: _____

Position(s): _____ Dates: _____

_____    _____

_____    _____

Description of responsibilities: _____

_____

_____

Contact name: _____ Phone: _____

Position: _____

## Previous Positions

Company: _____ Phone: _____

Address: _____

Position(s): _____ Dates: _____

_____    _____

_____    _____

Description of responsibilities: _____

_____

_____

Contact name: _____ Phone: _____

Position: _____

# RÉSUMÉ (CONTINUED)

Company: _____ Phone: _____

Address: _____

Position(s): _____ Dates: _____

_____    _____

_____    _____

Description of responsibilities: _____

_____

_____

Contact name: _____ Phone: _____

Position: _____

Company: _____ Phone: _____

Address: _____

Position(s): _____ Dates: _____

_____    _____

_____    _____

Description of responsibilities: _____

_____

_____

Contact name: _____ Phone: _____

Position: _____

# RÉSUMÉ (CONTINUED)

Company: _____ Phone: _____

Address: _____

Position(s): _____ Dates: _____

_____    _____

_____    _____

Description of responsibilities: _____

_____

_____

Contact name: _____ Phone: _____

Position: _____

## Community, religious, and volunteer involvement

| Name of Group | Work or position | Dates |
| --- | --- | --- |
| | | |
| | | |
| | | |
| | | |

## Special awards, recognitions, achievements: _____

_____

# CHILDREN'S SCHOOL RECORDS

Name: _____

Date of birth: _____ Social Security number: _____

School district: _____

School board contact(s):

_____ Phone: _____

_____ Phone: _____


Preschool: _____ Phone: _____

Address: _____

Dates of attendance: _____

Principal/Headmaster: _____

Teacher(s): _____


Kindergarten: _____ Phone: _____

Address: _____

Dates of attendance: _____

Principal/Headmaster: _____

Teacher(s): _____


Elementary school: _____ Phone: _____

Address: _____

Dates of attendance: _____

Principal/Headmaster: _____

Teacher(s): _____


Middle school: _____ Phone: _____

Address: _____

Dates of attendance: _____

Principal/Headmaster: _____

Teacher(s): _____


High school: _____ Phone: _____

Address: _____

Dates of attendance: _____

Principal/Headmaster: _____

Teachers—for references:

Name: _____ Phone: _____

Name: _____ Phone: _____

(Teacher references, continued)
Name: _____ Phone: _____
Name: _____ Phone: _____
Activities/offices held: _____

_____

Awards/honors: _____

_____

_____


College: _____ Phone: _____
Address: _____
Dates of attendance: _____
Major: _____ Minor: _____ Degree(s): _____
Teachers—for references:
Name: _____ Phone: _____
Name: _____ Phone: _____
Name: _____ Phone: _____
Name: _____ Phone: _____
Activities/offices held: _____

_____

Awards/honors: _____

_____

_____


College: _____ Phone: _____
Address: _____
Dates of attendance: _____
Major: _____ Minor: _____ Degree(s): _____
Teachers—for references:
Name: _____ Phone: _____
Name: _____ Phone: _____
Name: _____ Phone: _____
Name: _____ Phone: _____
Activities/offices held: _____

_____

Awards/honors: _____

_____

_____

# CHILDREN'S SCHOOL RECORDS

Name: _____

Date of birth: _____ Social Security number: _____

School district: _____

School board contact(s):

_____ Phone: _____

_____ Phone: _____


Preschool: _____ Phone: _____

Address: _____

Dates of attendance: _____

Principal/Headmaster: _____

Teacher(s): _____


Kindergarten: _____ Phone: _____

Address: _____

Dates of attendance: _____

Principal/Headmaster: _____

Teacher(s): _____


Elementary school: _____ Phone: _____

Address: _____

Dates of attendance: _____

Principal/Headmaster: _____

Teacher(s): _____


Middle school: _____ Phone: _____

Address: _____

Dates of attendance: _____

Principal/Headmaster: _____

Teacher(s): _____


High school: _____ Phone: _____

Address: _____

Dates of attendance: _____

Principal/Headmaster: _____

Teachers—for references:

Name: _____ Phone: _____

Name: _____ Phone: _____

(Teacher references, continued)

Name: _____ Phone: _____

Name: _____ Phone: _____

Activities/offices held: _____

_____

Awards/honors: _____

_____

_____

College: _____ Phone: _____

Address: _____

Dates of attendance: _____

Major: _____ Minor: _____ Degree(s): _____

Teachers—for references:

Name: _____ Phone: _____

Name: _____ Phone: _____

Name: _____ Phone: _____

Name: _____ Phone: _____

Activities/offices held: _____

_____

Awards/honors: _____

_____

_____

College: _____ Phone: _____

Address: _____

Dates of attendance: _____

Major: _____ Minor: _____ Degree(s): _____

Teachers—for references:

Name: _____ Phone: _____

Name: _____ Phone: _____

Name: _____ Phone: _____

Name: _____ Phone: _____

Activities/offices held: _____

_____

Awards/honors: _____

_____

_____

# CHILDREN'S SCHOOL RECORDS

Name: _____

Date of birth: _____ Social Security number: _____

School district: _____

School board contact(s):

_____ Phone: _____

_____ Phone: _____


Preschool: _____ Phone: _____

Address: _____

Dates of attendance: _____

Principal/Headmaster: _____

Teacher(s): _____


Kindergarten: _____ Phone: _____

Address: _____

Dates of attendance: _____

Principal/Headmaster: _____

Teacher(s): _____


Elementary school: _____ Phone: _____

Address: _____

Dates of attendance: _____

Principal/Headmaster: _____

Teacher(s): _____


Middle school: _____ Phone: _____

Address: _____

Dates of attendance: _____

Principal/Headmaster: _____

Teacher(s): _____


High school: _____ Phone: _____

Address: _____

Dates of attendance: _____

Principal/Headmaster: _____

Teachers—for references:

Name: _____ Phone: _____

Name: _____ Phone: _____

(Teacher references, continued)
Name: _____ Phone: _____
Name: _____ Phone: _____
Activities/offices held: _____
_____
_____

Awards/honors: _____
_____
_____

College: _____ Phone: _____
Address: _____
Dates of attendance: _____
Major: _____ Minor: _____ Degree(s): _____
Teachers—for references:
Name: _____ Phone: _____
Name: _____ Phone: _____
Name: _____ Phone: _____
Name: _____ Phone: _____
Activities/offices held: _____
_____
_____

Awards/honors: _____
_____
_____

College: _____ Phone: _____
Address: _____
Dates of attendance: _____
Major: _____ Minor: _____ Degree(s): _____
Teachers—for references:
Name: _____ Phone: _____
Name: _____ Phone: _____
Name: _____ Phone: _____
Name: _____ Phone: _____
Activities/offices held: _____
_____
_____

Awards/honors: _____
_____
_____

# CHILDREN'S SCHOOL RECORDS

Name: _____

Date of birth: _____ Social Security number: _____

School district: _____

School board contact(s):

_____ Phone: _____

_____ Phone: _____


Preschool: _____ Phone: _____

Address: _____

Dates of attendance: _____

Principal/Headmaster: _____

Teacher(s): _____


Kindergarten: _____ Phone: _____

Address: _____

Dates of attendance: _____

Principal/Headmaster: _____

Teacher(s): _____


Elementary school: _____ Phone: _____

Address: _____

Dates of attendance: _____

Principal/Headmaster: _____

Teacher(s): _____


Middle school: _____ Phone: _____

Address: _____

Dates of attendance: _____

Principal/Headmaster: _____

Teacher(s): _____


High school: _____ Phone: _____

Address: _____

Dates of attendance: _____

Principal/Headmaster: _____

Teachers—for references:

Name: _____ Phone: _____

Name: _____ Phone: _____

(Teacher references, continued)
Name: _____ Phone: _____
Name: _____ Phone: _____
Activities/offices held: _____

_____

Awards/honors: _____

_____

_____

College: _____ Phone: _____
Address: _____
Dates of attendance: _____
Major: _____ Minor: _____ Degree(s): _____
Teachers—for references:
Name: _____ Phone: _____
Name: _____ Phone: _____
Name: _____ Phone: _____
Name: _____ Phone: _____
Activities/offices held: _____

_____

Awards/honors: _____

_____

_____

College: _____ Phone: _____
Address: _____
Dates of attendance: _____
Major: _____ Minor: _____ Degree(s): _____
Teachers—for references:
Name: _____ Phone: _____
Name: _____ Phone: _____
Name: _____ Phone: _____
Name: _____ Phone: _____
Activities/offices held: _____

_____

Awards/honors: _____

_____

_____

# CHILDREN'S SCHEDULES

**Use this form to let your baby-sitter know your children's schedules.**

**Name of child:** _____

**Day:** _____

**School:** Contact person/Teacher: _____ Phone: _____

Begins      Ends      Transportation

_____ _____ _____

Items to be taken: _____

Special instructions: _____

**Activities:** Contact person: _____ Phone: _____

What      When      Transportation

_____ _____ _____

Location: _____ Map available, if needed: _____

Items to be taken: _____

Special instructions: _____

**Day:** _____

**School:** Contact person/Teacher: _____ Phone: _____

Begins      Ends      Transportation

_____ _____ _____

Items to be taken: _____

Special instructions: _____

**Activities:** Contact person: _____ Phone: _____

What      When      Transportation

_____ _____ _____

Location: _____ Map available, if needed: _____

Items to be taken: _____

Special instructions: _____

# CHILDREN'S SCHEDULES

**Use this form to let your baby-sitter know your children's schedules.**

**Name of child:** _____

**Day:** _____

  **School:** Contact person/Teacher: _____ Phone: _____

  <u>Begins</u>      <u>Ends</u>      <u>Transportation</u>

  _____ _____ _____

  Items to be taken: _____

  Special instructions: _____

  **Activities:** Contact person: _____ Phone: _____

  <u>What</u>      <u>When</u>      <u>Transportation</u>

  _____ _____ _____

  Location: _____ Map available, if needed: _____

  Items to be taken: _____

  Special instructions: _____

**Day:** _____

  **School:** Contact person/Teacher: _____ Phone: _____

  <u>Begins</u>      <u>Ends</u>      <u>Transportation</u>

  _____ _____ _____

  Items to be taken: _____

  Special instructions: _____

  **Activities:** Contact person: _____ Phone: _____

  <u>What</u>      <u>When</u>      <u>Transportation</u>

  _____ _____ _____

  Location: _____ Map available, if needed: _____

  Items to be taken: _____

  Special instructions: _____

# CHILDREN'S SCHEDULES

**Use this form to let your baby-sitter know your children's schedules.**

**Name of child:** _____

**Day:** _____

   **School:** Contact person/Teacher: _____ Phone: _____

   <u>Begins</u>     <u>Ends</u>     <u>Transportation</u>

   _____ _____ _____

   Items to be taken: _____

   Special instructions: _____

   **Activities:** Contact person: _____ Phone: _____

   <u>What</u>     <u>When</u>     <u>Transportation</u>

   _____ _____ _____

   Location: _____ Map available, if needed: _____

   Items to be taken: _____

   Special instructions: _____

**Day:** _____

   **School:** Contact person/Teacher: _____ Phone: _____

   <u>Begins</u>     <u>Ends</u>     <u>Transportation</u>

   _____ _____ _____

   Items to be taken: _____

   Special instructions: _____

   **Activities:** Contact person: _____ Phone: _____

   <u>What</u>     <u>When</u>     <u>Transportation</u>

   _____ _____ _____

   Location: _____ Map available, if needed: _____

   Items to be taken: _____

   Special instructions: _____

# CHILDREN'S SCHEDULES

**Use this form to let your baby-sitter know your children's schedules.**

**Name of child:** _____

**Day:** _____

  **School:** Contact person/Teacher: _____ Phone: _____

  <u>Begins</u>      <u>Ends</u>      <u>Transportation</u>

  _____ _____ _____

  Items to be taken: _____

  Special instructions: _____

  **Activities:** Contact person: _____ Phone: _____

  <u>What</u>      <u>When</u>      <u>Transportation</u>

  _____ _____ _____

  Location: _____ Map available, if needed: _____

  Items to be taken: _____

  Special instructions: _____

**Day:** _____

  **School:** Contact person/Teacher: _____ Phone: _____

  <u>Begins</u>      <u>Ends</u>      <u>Transportation</u>

  _____ _____ _____

  Items to be taken: _____

  Special instructions: _____

  **Activities:** Contact person: _____ Phone: _____

  <u>What</u>      <u>When</u>      <u>Transportation</u>

  _____ _____ _____

  Location: _____ Map available, if needed: _____

  Items to be taken: _____

  Special instructions: _____

# BABY-SITTER'S LOG

**Keep several copies of this form and the next handy, and complete it every time
you leave your children with a baby-sitter.**

Child's name: _____

Instructions for feeding: _____

_____

_____

_____

Allergic to: _____

Medications: _____

   Instructions for medications: _____

_____

_____

_____

TV programs children may/may not watch:

_____

_____

_____

_____

Rules: for homework: _____

_____

   for having friends over: _____

_____

   for bedtime: _____

To call in an emergency: _____

_____

# WHERE PARENTS AND OTHER RESPONSIBLE ADULTS CAN BE REACHED

Date                    Location                    Phone

_____         _____             _____

_____         _____             _____

_____         _____             _____

_____         _____             _____

_____         _____             _____

_____         _____             _____

_____         _____             _____

_____         _____             _____

_____         _____             _____

_____         _____             _____

_____         _____             _____

_____         _____             _____

_____         _____             _____

_____         _____             _____

_____         _____             _____

_____         _____             _____

_____         _____             _____

_____         _____             _____

_____         _____             _____

_____         _____             _____

# FAMILY BIRTHDAYS/ANNIVERSARIES

January

_____  _____

_____  _____

_____  _____

February

_____  _____

_____  _____

_____  _____

March

_____  _____

_____  _____

April

_____  _____

_____  _____

_____  _____

May

_____  _____

_____  _____

_____  _____

June

_____  _____

_____  _____

July

_____  _____

_____  _____

_____  _____

August

_____  _____

_____  _____

_____  _____

September

_____  _____

_____  _____

October

_____  _____

_____  _____

_____  _____

November

_____  _____

_____  _____

_____  _____

December

_____  _____

_____  _____

# OTHER IMPORTANT DATES TO REMEMBER

| Person(s) | Event | Date |
|-----------|-------|------|
|           |       |      |
|           |       |      |
|           |       |      |
|           |       |      |
|           |       |      |
|           |       |      |
|           |       |      |
|           |       |      |
|           |       |      |
|           |       |      |
|           |       |      |
|           |       |      |
|           |       |      |
|           |       |      |
|           |       |      |
|           |       |      |
|           |       |      |
|           |       |      |
|           |       |      |
|           |       |      |
|           |       |      |
|           |       |      |

# OTHER IMPORTANT DATES TO REMEMBER

| Person(s) | Event | Date |
|-----------|-------|------|
|           |       |      |
|           |       |      |
|           |       |      |
|           |       |      |
|           |       |      |
|           |       |      |
|           |       |      |
|           |       |      |
|           |       |      |
|           |       |      |
|           |       |      |
|           |       |      |
|           |       |      |
|           |       |      |
|           |       |      |
|           |       |      |
|           |       |      |
|           |       |      |
|           |       |      |
|           |       |      |
|           |       |      |
|           |       |      |
|           |       |      |

# VOLUNTEER AND COMMUNITY COMMITMENTS

Of: _____

## Name of organization: _____

Contact person: _____ Phone: _____

Contact person: _____ Phone: _____

Commitment/Responsibility: _____

Term of commitment: _____

Location of files/records: _____

Other pertinent information: _____

## Name of organization: _____

Contact person: _____ Phone: _____

Contact person: _____ Phone: _____

Commitment/Responsibility: _____

Term of commitment: _____

Location of files/records: _____

Other pertinent information: _____

## Name of organization: _____

Contact person: _____ Phone: _____

Contact person: _____ Phone: _____

Commitment/Responsibility: _____

Term of commitment: _____

Location of files/records: _____

Other pertinent information: _____

# VOLUNTEER AND COMMUNITY COMMITMENTS

Of: _____

**Name of organization:** _____

Contact person: _____ Phone: _____

Contact person: _____ Phone: _____

Commitment/Responsibility: _____

Term of commitment: _____

Location of files/records: _____

Other pertinent information: _____

**Name of organization:** _____

Contact person: _____ Phone: _____

Contact person: _____ Phone: _____

Commitment/Responsibility: _____

Term of commitment: _____

Location of files/records: _____

Other pertinent information: _____

**Name of organization:** _____

Contact person: _____ Phone: _____

Contact person: _____ Phone: _____

Commitment/Responsibility: _____

Term of commitment: _____

Location of files/records: _____

Other pertinent information: _____

# OTHER NAMES AND ADDRESSES

This is a sample format that I have used on a database on my computer. While a computer makes this easier, this format could be adapted to use on a 3 × 5 card. A little explanation may help make sense out of some portions of the form. I like to know when I initially entered someone on my database, and I have found it helpful to know when information was last changed. The location indicates if it is business, residential, second home, etc. For salutation I put "Mr. & Mrs. John D." or "Dr. & Mrs. John D." or "Dear John and Mary." I admit that the Special Code gets a little trickier, but makes life easier. I enter a two-letter code that provides a quick way to sort. For example, XC represents those on my Christmas card list; SR is for all of those who provide service or repair, like my plumber; TH and TR remind me of a great hotel or restaurant in a particular city; FA is family; and so on. Use your imagination. Many entries have multiple-use codes so they can be included in multiple lists. The comments section allows room for all of that miscellaneous information that does not fit anywhere else such as a former maiden name, occupation, or who made the referral.

Date of entry: _____ Last change: _____ Location: _____

Last name: _____ First name: _____

Salutation (Dr., Mr., Mrs., Ms., etc.): _____

Address: _____

_____

City: _____ State: _____ Zip: _____

Phone—Home: _____ Mobile: _____ Office: _____

Fax: _____ E-mail: _____

Salutation: _____

Spouse: _____ Children: _____

_____

Birth dates: _____

Special Code: _____

Comments: _____

_____

_____

_____

# TRAVEL ITINERARY

**Complete this form and leave several copies with family and friends every time you travel.**

Person(s) traveling: _____

Method:  Air _____ Car _____ Ship _____ Other: _____

Frequent Flier Account #: _____

Departure—Date: _____ Carrier: _____ Flight #: _____

Carrier: _____ Flight #: _____

Carrier: _____ Flight #: _____

Arrival at destination—Date: _____ Time: _____

Method of transportation to hotel: Taxi _____ Hotel van _____ Rental car _____

If rental car, company: _____ Confirmation #: _____

Personal or corporate discount #: _____

Being met by: _____ Phone #: _____

Where being met: _____

Accommodations: _____

| Hotel | Address | Dates | Phone/Fax |
|-------|---------|-------|-----------|
| _____ | _____ | _____ | _____ |
| _____ | _____ | _____ | _____ |
| _____ | _____ | _____ | _____ |
| _____ | _____ | _____ | _____ |

Return—Date: _____ Carrier: _____ Flight #: _____

Carrier: _____ Flight #: _____

Carrier: _____ Flight #: _____

Arrival at home—Date: _____ Time: _____

Method of transportation home: Car _____ Taxi _____

Being met by: _____ Phone #: _____

Where being met: _____

Special instructions/Information: _____

_____

# PACKING CHECKLIST

## General List

- [ ] Tickets
- [ ] Passport
- [ ] Visas
- [ ] Wallet with necessary credit cards
- [ ] Traveler's checks
- [ ] Itinerary—complete with all addresses, phone numbers, confirmation numbers
- [ ] Copy of medical history
- [ ] Duplicate prescriptions
- [ ] Medicines
    - [ ] Prescription
    - [ ] Over-the-counter
    - [ ] Vitamins

- [ ] Camera/film
- [ ] Umbrella
- [ ] Glasses/Sunglasses
- [ ] Books
- [ ] Business cards

- [ ] First-aid supplies
- [ ] Alarm clock
- [ ] Comb/brush
- [ ] Deodorant
- [ ] Toothbrush/paste
- [ ] Mouthwash
- [ ] Dental floss
- [ ] Shampoo/conditioner
- [ ] Styling gel/mousse
- [ ] Hairspray
- [ ] Sunblock
- [ ] Nail clippers
- [ ] Tweezers
- [ ] Detergent/spot remover
- [ ] Small sewing kit with needle, thread, buttons, scissors, pins—safety and straight
- [ ] Adapters/converter 110v/220v
- [ ] Hairdryer

**For him:** [ ] shaving supplies
**For her:** [ ] makeup
   [ ] perfume
   [ ] nail file, polish and remover
   [ ] sanitary supplies
   [ ] mirror
   [ ] razor
   [ ] curling iron

## Leave at home:

- [ ] Copy of itinerary
- [ ] Copy of passport
- [ ] Copy of traveler's check #'s
- [ ] Unneeded credit cards

# PACKING CHECKLIST (CONTINUED)

## His List

- ☐ Suits
- ☐ Jackets
- ☐ Slacks
- ☐ Shorts
- ☐ Shirts
    - ☐ Dress
    - ☐ Casual
- ☐ Ties
- ☐ Belts
- ☐ Shoes
    - ☐ Dress
    - ☐ Casual
    - ☐ Exercise
- ☐ Swimsuit/water shoes
- ☐ Exercise clothes
- ☐ Pajamas/robe/slippers
- ☐ Underwear
- ☐ Socks
    - ☐ Dress
    - ☐ Athletic
- ☐ Sweaters
- ☐ Hats
- ☐ Gloves
- ☐ Coat/raincoat
- ☐ Handkerchiefs
- ☐ Cuff links/tie clasps

## Her List

- ☐ Suits
- ☐ Jackets
- ☐ Skirts
- ☐ Slacks
- ☐ Shorts
- ☐ Blouses
- ☐ Dresses
- ☐ Jewelry
- ☐ Belts
- ☐ Shoes
    - ☐ Dress
    - ☐ Casual
    - ☐ Exercise
- ☐ Swimsuit/water shoes/cover-up
- ☐ Exercise clothes
- ☐ Gown or pajamas/robe/slippers
- ☐ Lingerie
- ☐ Hose/socks
- ☐ Sweaters
- ☐ Scarves/handkerchiefs
- ☐ Hats
- ☐ Gloves
- ☐ Coat/raincoat
- ☐ Purses

Remember to put your name/address/phone number inside and outside your luggage.

*Think* before you pack—coordinate. Take *only* what you need. Resist the temptation to overpack.

Put anything that may leak in Ziploc bags. Put in an extra plastic bag for a wet swimsuit.

# CLOTHING SIZES

## Men

**Name:** _____

Neck: _____ Chest: _____ Shirt: _____ Sleeve: _____

Suit: _____ Waist: _____ Inseam: _____ Hat: _____

Pajamas: _____ Undershirt: _____ Undershorts: _____

Sweater: _____ Gloves: _____ Shoes: _____ Socks: _____

Belt: _____

**Name:** _____

Neck: _____ Chest: _____ Shirt: _____ Sleeve: _____

Suit: _____ Waist: _____ Inseam: _____ Hat: _____

Pajamas: _____ Undershirt: _____ Undershorts: _____

Sweater: _____ Gloves: _____ Shoes: _____ Socks: _____

Belt: _____

**Name:** _____

Neck: _____ Chest: _____ Shirt: _____ Sleeve: _____

Suit: _____ Waist: _____ Inseam: _____ Hat: _____

Pajamas: _____ Undershirt: _____ Undershorts: _____

Sweater: _____ Gloves: _____ Shoes: _____ Socks: _____

Belt: _____

**Name:** _____

Neck: _____ Chest: _____ Shirt: _____ Sleeve: _____

Suit: _____ Waist: _____ Inseam: _____ Hat: _____

Pajamas: _____ Undershirt: _____ Undershorts: _____

Sweater: _____ Gloves: _____ Shoes: _____ Socks: _____

Belt: _____

# CLOTHING SIZES

## Women

**Name:** _____

Dress: _____ Jacket: _____ Skirt: _____

Blouse: _____ Sweater: _____

Gown/pj's: _____ Robe: _____ Lingerie: _____ Hat: _____

Shoes: _____ Hose: _____ Socks: _____ Gloves: _____

Belt: _____ Earrings: Pierced _____ Clip _____

**Name:** _____

Dress: _____ Jacket: _____ Skirt: _____

Blouse: _____ Sweater: _____

Gown/pj's: _____ Robe: _____ Lingerie: _____ Hat: _____

Shoes: _____ Hose: _____ Socks: _____ Gloves: _____

Belt: _____ Earrings: Pierced _____ Clip _____

**Name:** _____

Dress: _____ Jacket: _____ Skirt: _____

Blouse: _____ Sweater: _____

Gown/pj's: _____ Robe: _____ Lingerie: _____ Hat: _____

Shoes: _____ Hose: _____ Socks: _____ Gloves: _____

Belt: _____ Earrings: Pierced _____ Clip _____

**Name:** _____

Dress: _____ Jacket: _____ Skirt: _____

Blouse: _____ Sweater: _____

Gown/pj's: _____ Robe: _____ Lingerie: _____ Hat: _____

Shoes: _____ Hose: _____ Socks: _____ Gloves: _____

Belt: _____ Earrings: Pierced _____ Clip _____

# PET RECORDS

**Pet emergency clinic:** _____ Phone: _____

    Location: _____

    Directions: _____

Location of extra food: _____

**Name:** _____ Date of birth: _____

Type of animal: _____ Breed: _____

Veterinarian: _____ Phone: _____

    Address: _____

Food/Feeding schedule: _____

Date of last shots: _____ When next shots are due: _____

Groomer: _____ Phone: _____

Boarding: _____ Phone: _____

**Name:** _____ Date of birth: _____

Type of animal: _____ Breed: _____

Veterinarian: _____ Phone: _____

    Address: _____

Food/Feeding schedule: _____

Date of last shots: _____ When next shots are due: _____

Groomer: _____ Phone: _____

Boarding: _____ Phone: _____

**Name:** _____ Date of birth: _____

Type of animal: _____ Breed: _____

Veterinarian: _____ Phone: _____

    Address: _____

Food/Feeding schedule: _____

Date of last shots: _____ When next shots are due: _____

Groomer: _____ Phone: _____

Boarding: _____ Phone: _____

# PET RECORDS

**Pet emergency clinic:** _____ Phone: _____
  Location: _____
  Directions: _____
Location of extra food: _____

**Name:** _____ Date of birth: _____
Type of animal: _____ Breed: _____
Veterinarian: _____ Phone: _____
  Address: _____
Food/Feeding schedule: _____
Date of last shots: _____ When next shots are due: _____
Groomer: _____ Phone: _____
Boarding: _____ Phone: _____

**Name:** _____ Date of birth: _____
Type of animal: _____ Breed: _____
Veterinarian: _____ Phone: _____
  Address: _____
Food/Feeding schedule: _____
Date of last shots: _____ When next shots are due: _____
Groomer: _____ Phone: _____
Boarding: _____ Phone: _____

**Name:** _____ Date of birth: _____
Type of animal: _____ Breed: _____
Veterinarian: _____ Phone: _____
  Address: _____
Food/Feeding schedule: _____
Date of last shots: _____ When next shots are due: _____
Groomer: _____ Phone: _____
Boarding: _____ Phone: _____

# FUNERAL AND BURIAL INSTRUCTIONS

For: _____

Person(s) recommended to make decisions regarding details:

Name: _____ Phone: _____

Name: _____ Phone: _____

Name: _____ Phone: _____

Funeral home preference: _____

   Address: _____ Phone: _____

   Casket preferred: _____

   Visitation with family—Funeral home: _____

      Private home: _____

      Other: _____

Prior arrangements: _____

Prefer: Burial _____ Cremation _____ Donate to science _____

Open casket: _____ Closed casket: _____

Special requests (e.g., jewelry): _____

_____

Place of burial—Cemetery: _____

   Address: _____

   Contact: _____ Phone: _____

   Plot owned? Location of deed: _____

     If not, type preferred: _____

   If cremation, wishes regarding placement of ashes: _____

Wishes regarding headstone: _____

Wishes regarding type of service:

Funeral: _____ Memorial service: _____ Graveside only: _____

Masonic: _____ Military: _____ Other: _____

Where is the service to be held?

Church: _____ Phone: _____

    Address: _____

Funeral home: _____

Other: _____

Who is to officiate? _____ Phone: _____

Structure of service: _____

    If you have planned your own service, where are the instructions located?

    _____

    Scripture requests: _____

    Music requests: _____

    Other: _____

Wishes regarding contributions or donations: _____

_____

Wishes regarding flowers after service—On grave: _____

Given to shut-ins/others: _____

Other: _____

Special requests/concerns: _____

_____

_____

# PALLBEARER INFORMATION

For: _____

Name: _____ Phone: _____

Address: _____ Active: _____ Honorary: _____

Name: _____ Phone: _____

Address: _____ Active: _____ Honorary: _____

Name: _____ Phone: _____

Address: _____ Active: _____ Honorary: _____

Name: _____ Phone: _____

Address: _____ Active: _____ Honorary: _____

Name: _____ Phone: _____

Address: _____ Active: _____ Honorary: _____

Name: _____ Phone: _____

Address: _____ Active: _____ Honorary: _____

Name: _____ Phone: _____

Address: _____ Active: _____ Honorary: _____

Name: _____ Phone: _____

Address: _____ Active: _____ Honorary: _____

Name: _____ Phone: _____

Address: _____ Active: _____ Honorary: _____

Name: _____ Phone: _____

Address: _____ Active: _____ Honorary: _____

# NOTIFY IN CASE OF DEATH

Name: _____ Relationship: _____

Address: _____ Phone: _____

Name: _____ Relationship: _____

Address: _____ Phone: _____

Name: _____ Relationship: _____

Address: _____ Phone: _____

Name: _____ Relationship: _____

Address: _____ Phone: _____

Name: _____ Relationship: _____

Address: _____ Phone: _____

Name: _____ Relationship: _____

Address: _____ Phone: _____

Name: _____ Relationship: _____

Address: _____ Phone: _____

Name: _____ Relationship: _____

Address: _____ Phone: _____

Name: _____ Relationship: _____

Address: _____ Phone: _____

Name: _____ Relationship: _____

Address: _____ Phone: _____

Name: _____ Relationship: _____

Address: _____ Phone: _____

# INSTRUCTIONS FOR DISTRIBUTION

In addition to my will and any codicil that may exist, I wish to designate that the following items be given to the indicated individual:

Item: _____ Individual: _____

Item: _____ Individual: _____

Item: _____ Individual: _____

Item: _____ Individual: _____

Item: _____ Individual: _____

Item: _____ Individual: _____

Item: _____ Individual: _____

Item: _____ Individual: _____

Item: _____ Individual: _____

Item: _____ Individual: _____

Item: _____ Individual: _____

Item: _____ Individual: _____

Item: _____ Individual: _____

Item: _____ Individual: _____

Item: _____ Individual: _____

Item: _____ Individual: _____

Item: _____ Individual: _____

Item: _____ Individual: _____

Item: _____ Individual: _____

Item: _____ Individual: _____

Item: _____ Individual: _____

Item: _____ Individual: _____

Date: _____   _____

(Signature)

# FUNERAL AND BURIAL INSTRUCTIONS

For: _____

Person(s) recommended to make decisions regarding details:

Name: _____ Phone: _____

Name: _____ Phone: _____

Name: _____ Phone: _____

Funeral home preference: _____

    Address: _____ Phone: _____

    Casket preferred: _____

    Visitation with family—Funeral home: _____

        Private home: _____

        Other: _____

Prior arrangements: _____

Prefer: Burial _____ Cremation _____ Donate to science _____

Open casket: _____ Closed casket: _____

Special requests (e.g., jewelry): _____

_____

Place of burial—Cemetery: _____

    Address: _____

    Contact: _____ Phone: _____

    Plot owned? Location of deed: _____

        If not, type preferred: _____

    If cremation, wishes regarding placement of ashes: _____

Wishes regarding headstone: _____

Wishes regarding type of service:

Funeral: _____ Memorial service: _____ Graveside only: _____

Masonic: _____ Military: _____ Other: _____

Where is the service to be held?

Church: _____ Phone: _____

    Address: _____

Funeral home: _____

Other: _____

Who is to officiate? _____ Phone: _____

Structure of service: _____

    If you have planned your own service, where are the instructions located?

    _____

    Scripture requests: _____

    Music requests: _____

    Other: _____

Wishes regarding contributions or donations: _____

_____

Wishes regarding flowers after service—On grave: _____

Given to shut-ins/others: _____

Other: _____

Special requests/concerns: _____

_____

_____

# PALLBEARER INFORMATION

For: _____

Name: _____ Phone: _____

Address: _____ Active: _____ Honorary: _____

Name: _____ Phone: _____

Address: _____ Active: _____ Honorary: _____

Name: _____ Phone: _____

Address: _____ Active: _____ Honorary: _____

Name: _____ Phone: _____

Address: _____ Active: _____ Honorary: _____

Name: _____ Phone: _____

Address: _____ Active: _____ Honorary: _____

Name: _____ Phone: _____

Address: _____ Active: _____ Honorary: _____

Name: _____ Phone: _____

Address: _____ Active: _____ Honorary: _____

Name: _____ Phone: _____

Address: _____ Active: _____ Honorary: _____

Name: _____ Phone: _____

Address: _____ Active: _____ Honorary: _____

Name: _____ Phone: _____

Address: _____ Active: _____ Honorary: _____

# NOTIFY IN CASE OF DEATH

Name: _____ Relationship: _____

Address: _____ Phone: _____

Name: _____ Relationship: _____

Address: _____ Phone: _____

Name: _____ Relationship: _____

Address: _____ Phone: _____

Name: _____ Relationship: _____

Address: _____ Phone: _____

Name: _____ Relationship: _____

Address: _____ Phone: _____

Name: _____ Relationship: _____

Address: _____ Phone: _____

Name: _____ Relationship: _____

Address: _____ Phone: _____

Name: _____ Relationship: _____

Address: _____ Phone: _____

Name: _____ Relationship: _____

Address: _____ Phone: _____

Name: _____ Relationship: _____

Address: _____ Phone: _____

Name: _____ Relationship: _____

Address: _____ Phone: _____

Name: _____ Relationship: _____

Address: _____ Phone: _____

# INSTRUCTIONS FOR DISTRIBUTION

In addition to my will and any codicil that may exist, I wish to designate that the following items be given to the indicated individual:

Item: _____ Individual: _____

Item: _____ Individual: _____

Item: _____ Individual: _____

Item: _____ Individual: _____

Item: _____ Individual: _____

Item: _____ Individual: _____

Item: _____ Individual: _____

Item: _____ Individual: _____

Item: _____ Individual: _____

Item: _____ Individual: _____

Item: _____ Individual: _____

Item: _____ Individual: _____

Item: _____ Individual: _____

Item: _____ Individual: _____

Item: _____ Individual: _____

Item: _____ Individual: _____

Item: _____ Individual: _____

Item: _____ Individual: _____

Item: _____ Individual: _____

Item: _____ Individual: _____

Item: _____ Individual: _____

Item: _____ Individual: _____

Item: _____ Individual: _____

Date: _____        _____
                                                    (Signature)

# YOUR HOME

Just in case you need more convincing or reassurance that most of this information is really needed, think through the times of your life when you needed some information and couldn't remember where in the world you had filed it. Imagine trying to remember where that water cutoff valve is when your kitchen is being flooded. Who was that painter you liked so much, and who cleaned up so nicely when he finished? Where is your safe deposit box? Your birth certificates? Your will?

What if you are unavailable? What if you are out of town on business? What if you have been injured in a car wreck and cannot explain where anything is? Do others in your family have access to critical information? As a banker, I encountered many distraught individuals who didn't know where a safe deposit box was located, the status of accounts, or what loans existed. In our home, pipes have frozen when my husband and I were out of town on business, and a baby/house sitter needed to handle the crisis.

Some of this information is extremely critical in times of emergencies, while some of it will simply be handy to have on hand for everyday use. By taking a little time to complete and maintain *The Essential Home Record Book*, I guarantee that in the long run you will save considerable time and hassle in your life.

Now for some helpful hints to assist you in completing the Home section. For some pages, such as the emergency and important number list, you may want additional copies to keep with phone directories in various places in your home. While you are at it, if you have small children, make an extra copy of that number list for the baby-sitter. Complete customer-service numbers for appliances, televisions, etc., as you buy them. For easy access to instructions for these items, create a file, or a drawer of files, for all instructions and warranties. I even staple receipts to the instructions so I will have the merchant and date information readily accessible for warranty claims. A word of caution: Be sure to update information when you move, when new neighbors move in, or when you change doctors or advisers. Remember, maintenance is easy one name or number at a time.

When you complete the home computer page, pretend you are explaining "how to" to the most computer-illiterate members of the family. Also, a word to the wise: If you have everything on a computer and see no reason for a "hard copy," remember you may have a computer-illiterate family member who could not access information in an emergency. Or the power could go off. The bottom line is make a hard copy just in case.

# LOCATION OF IMPORTANT DOCUMENTS

Appointment calendar: _____

Appraisals—Antiques/Art/Jewelry/etc.: _____

Birth certificates: _____

_____

Baptismal certificates: _____

_____

Car maintenance/repair/warranty: _____

Car titles/registrations: _____

_____

Cemetery deed: _____

Death certificate: _____

Diplomas: _____

Divorce/Separation documents: _____

Employment records: _____

Financial records: Bank statements—Current year: _____

Prior years: _____

Payables: _____

Receipts: _____

Receivables: _____

Other: _____

Financial statements: _____

Home inventory: _____

Income tax returns: _____ Insurance policies: _____

Investment files: _____ IRA/Keogh/401K: _____

Loan/Mortgage/Lease agreements: _____

Copyright © 1997 Pamela K. Pfeffer

Marriage certificate: _____

Medical receipts/Insurance payments: _____

Medical records: _____

Military discharge records, etc.: _____

Passport: _____

_____

Real estate documents: _____

_____

Safe deposit box: _____

Trust: _____

_____

Will: _____

_____

Other: _____

_____

_____

_____

_____

_____

_____

_____

_____

_____

_____

_____

# COMPUTER FILE RECORDS

Password: _____

Computer consultant: _____ Phone: _____

To access:

Address and phone files: _____

_____

_____

_____

_____

Financial data: _____

_____

_____

_____

_____

Correspondence: _____

_____

_____

_____

_____

Other: _____

_____

_____

_____

_____

# IMPORTANT UTILITY LOCATIONS

Alarm main control box and system-control pads(s): _____

_____

_____

Code #: _____ Security code #: _____

Carbon-monoxide detector location(s): _____

_____

Electrical circuit-breaker box(es): _____

Gas cutoff: _____

Pipeline location: _____

Keys—Alarm: _____

Bar: _____

Boat: _____

Car(s): _____

Hidden keys: _____

House: _____

Safe deposit box: _____

_____

_____

Safe—Location: _____ Combination: _____

Smoke-detector location(s): _____

_____

Thermostat(s): _____

Water cutoff—Inside: _____

Outside: _____

Sprinkler: _____

Pool: _____

Other: _____

# HOME MAINTENANCE LOG

| Service | Company | Phone Number | Schedule | Last Serviced |
|---|---|---|---|---|
| Alarm | | | | |
| Appliances | | | | |
|   Ice maker | _____ | _____ | _____ | _____ |
|   Oven/Stove | _____ | _____ | _____ | _____ |
|   Refrigerator/Freezer | _____ | _____ | _____ | _____ |
|   Small appliances | _____ | _____ | _____ | _____ |
|   Stereo | _____ | _____ | _____ | _____ |
|   Television | _____ | _____ | _____ | _____ |
|   Washer/Dryer | _____ | _____ | _____ | _____ |
| Cable company | _____ | _____ | _____ | _____ |
| Carpenter | _____ | _____ | _____ | _____ |
| Computer repair | _____ | _____ | _____ | _____ |
| Dairy | _____ | _____ | _____ | _____ |
| Deliveries | _____ | _____ | _____ | _____ |
| Electrician | _____ | _____ | _____ | _____ |
| Garbage collection | _____ | _____ | _____ | _____ |
| Heating/Air conditioner | _____ | _____ | _____ | _____ |
| House cleaning | _____ | _____ | _____ | _____ |
| Locksmith | _____ | _____ | _____ | _____ |
| Newspaper delivery | _____ | _____ | _____ | _____ |
| Painter | _____ | _____ | _____ | _____ |
| Pest control | _____ | _____ | _____ | _____ |
| Plumber | _____ | _____ | _____ | _____ |
|   Drain cleaner | _____ | _____ | _____ | _____ |
| Pool service | _____ | _____ | _____ | _____ |
| Snow removal | _____ | _____ | _____ | _____ |
| Wallpaper hanger | _____ | _____ | _____ | _____ |
| Window cleaner | _____ | _____ | _____ | _____ |
| Yard | | | | |
|   Cutting | _____ | _____ | _____ | _____ |
|   Landscaping | _____ | _____ | _____ | _____ |
|   Lawn care | _____ | _____ | _____ | _____ |
|   Tree surgeon | _____ | _____ | _____ | _____ |
| Other | | | | |
| _____ | _____ | _____ | _____ | _____ |
| _____ | _____ | _____ | _____ | _____ |

# PERSONAL SERVICES

Baby-sitters

   Name: _____ Address: _____ Phone: _____

   Name: _____ Address: _____ Phone: _____

   Name: _____ Address: _____ Phone: _____

   Name: _____ Address: _____ Phone: _____

Car service/Taxi: _____ Phone(s): _____

Carpool—Names/Phones: _____

Church: _____ Address: _____ Phone: _____

   Clergy: _____ Phone: _____

Clothing

   Dry cleaner:_____ Address: _____ Phone: _____

   Shoe repair: _____ Address: _____ Phone: _____

   Tailor:_____ Address: _____ Phone: _____

Country club/Racquet club: _____

   Address: _____ Phone: _____

Gym: _____ Address: _____

   Personal trainer: _____ Phone: _____

Hair: _____ Address: _____ Phone: _____

Nails: _____ Address: _____ Phone: _____

Pet

   Groomer: _____ Address: _____ Phone: _____

   Sitter/Walker: _____ Address: _____ Phone: _____

   Veterinarian: _____ Address: _____ Phone: _____

Other

   _____ Address: _____ Phone: _____

   _____ Address: _____ Phone: _____

   _____ Address: _____ Phone: _____

   _____ Address: _____ Phone: _____

   _____ Address: _____ Phone: _____

   _____ Address: _____ Phone: _____

## APPLIANCE CHECKLIST

| Appliances | Brand | Model Number/ Serial Number | Date of Purchase | Term of Warranty | Service or Manufacturer's Phone Number |
|---|---|---|---|---|---|
| Dishwasher | | | | | |
| Disposal | | | | | |
| Ice maker | | | | | |
| Microwave | | | | | |
| Oven | | | | | |
| Stove | | | | | |
| Refrigerator | | | | | |
| Freezer | | | | | |
| Trash compactor | | | | | |
| Washer | | | | | |
| Dryer | | | | | |
| | | | | | |
| | | | | | |
| | | | | | |

# APPLIANCE CHECKLIST (CONTINUED)

| Appliances | Brand | Model Number/ Serial Number | Date of Purchase | Term of Warranty | Service or Manufacturer's Phone Number |
|---|---|---|---|---|---|
| **HEATING AND AIR CONDITIONING/WATER HEATER** | | | | | |
| Air conditioner(s) | | | | | |
| Furnace(s) | | | | | |
| Humidifier(s) | | | | | |
| Water heater(s) | | | | | |
| | | | | | |
| **TELEVISION/STEREO/VCR/CD/ETC.** | | | | | |
| CD | | | | | |
| Stereo(s) | | | | | |
| Television(s) | | | | | |
| VCR | | | | | |

# APPLIANCE CHECKLIST (CONTINUED)

| Appliances | Brand | Model Number/ Serial Number | Date of Purchase | Term of Warranty | Service or Manufacturer's Phone Number |
|---|---|---|---|---|---|
| **HOME OFFICE** | | | | | |
| Answering machine | | | | | |
| Computer | | | | | |
| Copier | | | | | |
| Fax | | | | | |
| Printer | | | | | |
| | | | | | |
| | | | | | |
| **OTHER** | | | | | |
| | | | | | |
| | | | | | |
| | | | | | |

# HOME INSPECTION CHECKLIST

| What | Who Does It? | Last Inspection | Next Inspection Due |
|------|--------------|-----------------|---------------------|
| Alarm | _____ | _____ | _____ |
| Carbon-monoxide (CO) detectors | _____ | _____ | _____ |
| Filters | | | |
|    Furnace | _____ | _____ | _____ |
|    Humidifiers | _____ | _____ | _____ |
|    Spa | _____ | _____ | _____ |
| Fireplace/Chimney | _____ | _____ | _____ |
| Heat/A/C | _____ | _____ | _____ |
| Pool | _____ | _____ | _____ |
| Smoke detectors | _____ | _____ | _____ |
| Sprinklers | _____ | _____ | _____ |
| Termite | _____ | _____ | _____ |
| _____ | _____ | _____ | _____ |
| _____ | _____ | _____ | _____ |
| _____ | _____ | _____ | _____ |
| _____ | _____ | _____ | _____ |
| _____ | _____ | _____ | _____ |
| _____ | _____ | _____ | _____ |
| _____ | _____ | _____ | _____ |
| _____ | _____ | _____ | _____ |
| _____ | _____ | _____ | _____ |
| _____ | _____ | _____ | _____ |
| _____ | _____ | _____ | _____ |

# RECYCLING INFORMATION*

Recycling Collection
Phone Number: _____

| What | Preparation | Location | When Collected |
|---|---|---|---|
| Aluminum | Empty contents, rinse | | |
| Cans—steel and bi-metal ("tin") | Rinse (free of food), labels OK, flatten | | |
| Cardboard (corrugated only) | Open flat, stack (includes brown grocery bags) | | |
| Catalogs | Dry, stapled | | |
| Glass | Rinse, separate by color, labels OK, remove caps | | |
| Magazines | Dry | | |
| Paper—Computer | Dry, remove staples, etc. Separate laser from dot matrix ink | | |
| Newspaper | Dry, in bundles, inserts OK | | |
| Office paper | Dry, remove staples, etc. Check local market—may need to separate types of paper | | |

*Always check with your local recycling service for special instructions and current requirements.

Copyright © 1997 Pamela K. Pfeffer

# RECYCLING (CONTINUED)

| What | Preparation | Location | When Collected |
|------|-------------|----------|----------------|
| Plastic—Bags | Separate containers at grocery stores and dry cleaners only | | |
| Jugs (juice, milk) (No. 2 HDPE) | Rinse, remove caps, labels OK | | |
| Soda bottles (No. 1, PET) | Rinse, remove caps, labels OK | | |
| Telephone directory | Dry | | |
| Other | | | |
| | | | |
| | | | |
| | | | |

For local recycling information call:

| | | |
|--|--|--|
| Aluminum | The Aluminum Association | (202) 862-5100 |
| Glass | Glass Packaging | (317) 282-1603 |
| Paper | American Forest and Paper Association | (800) 878-8878 |
| Plastics | American Plastics Council | (800) 243-5790 |
| Steel | Steel Recycling Institute | (800) 876-7274 |

Copyright © 1997 Pamela K. Pfeffer

# EMERGENCY NUMBERS AT VACATION HOME

Address: _____ Zip: _____

Phone: _____, _____ Fax: _____

Directions from nearest highway: _____

_____

_____

_____

Key location(s): _____

Others who have keys: _____

Management company: _____ Phone: _____

Address: _____ Contact: _____

Neighbor: _____

Address: _____

Home: _____ Office: _____ Mobile: _____

Neighbor: _____

Address: _____

Home: _____ Office: _____ Mobile: _____

Fire: _____ Police: _____

Ambulance: _____ Pet emergency: _____

Poison control: _____ Alarm company: _____

Hospital name: _____

Address: _____

Directions: _____

_____

# HOME INVENTORY RECORDS

Room or Group of Items: _____

| Item Description | Purchase Date | New or Est. Age | Original or Est. Value | Appraised Value | Appraisal Date |
|---|---|---|---|---|---|
| | | | | | |
| | | | | | |
| | | | | | |
| | | | | | |
| | | | | | |
| | | | | | |
| | | | | | |
| | | | | | |
| | | | | | |
| | | | | | |
| | | | | | |

# HOME INVENTORY RECORDS

Room or Group of Items: _____

| Item Description | Purchase Date | New or Est. Age | Original or Est. Value | Appraised Value | Appraisal Date |
|---|---|---|---|---|---|
| | | | | | |
| | | | | | |
| | | | | | |
| | | | | | |
| | | | | | |
| | | | | | |
| | | | | | |
| | | | | | |
| | | | | | |
| | | | | | |
| | | | | | |
| | | | | | |
| | | | | | |
| | | | | | |

# HOME INVENTORY RECORDS

Room or Group of Items: _____

| Item Description | Purchase Date | New or Est. Age | Original or Est. Value | Appraised Value | Appraisal Date |
|---|---|---|---|---|---|
| | | | | | |
| | | | | | |
| | | | | | |
| | | | | | |
| | | | | | |
| | | | | | |
| | | | | | |
| | | | | | |
| | | | | | |
| | | | | | |
| | | | | | |
| | | | | | |

# HOME INVENTORY RECORDS

Room or Group of Items: _____

| Item Description | Purchase Date | New or Est. Age | Original or Est. Value | Appraised Value | Appraisal Date |
|---|---|---|---|---|---|
| | | | | | |
| | | | | | |
| | | | | | |
| | | | | | |
| | | | | | |
| | | | | | |
| | | | | | |
| | | | | | |
| | | | | | |
| | | | | | |
| | | | | | |
| | | | | | |
| | | | | | |

# MEDICAL RECORDS

What if you are out of town on business and your child is sledding when a tree just "jumps out" in front of him, smashing the sled, and possibly his shoulder? Who is authorized to obtain medical care for him? When did he last have a tetanus shot? Is he allergic to any medicine?

For *each minor* in your family, complete a consent form for emergency treatment. Authorize people that you trust, who are able to handle crises, and who are available to step in in an emergency. While your signature does not always have to be notarized, it does eliminate questions of proper authority in a time of crisis. Since hospitals normally require insurance information, be sure to include information regarding insurance.

Complete a copy of the medical history for *each* member of the family or household. This can quickly provide necessary information for a doctor. Even in non-crisis times, this information can be handy. I cannot begin to count the number of times I have needed to complete forms for my children giving permission to go camping with the Boy Scouts, or to participate in a school or church event. My children all too often wait until the last second to have me sign the forms. Quick access to the date of the last tetanus shot has proven to be an invaluable time saver. Also, make an extra copy of your medical history to take with you when you travel. You may never need it away from home, but it could prove invaluable. It may even save your life.

With the advances in modern medicine, doctors can often prolong life with the use of machinery. If you have strong feelings regarding your care using these life-prolonging measures, then you need to state them in a living will. I also recommend that you have everyone in the family think through his or her feelings, before a crisis, and sign a living will. While the form that is provided covers the basics, laws vary from state to state and from year to year. I urge you to consult with your attorney for the legal requirements in your area. Nonetheless, this generic form at least gives you the opportunity to discuss your feelings within your family, and gives a strong indication of your preferences to your doctors should a crisis occur. And for further evidence of your intentions, have your living will notarized. For more information regarding standard forms and procedures for each state, you may contact Choice in Dying at 200 Varick Street, New York, NY 10014, 212-366-5540, or toll-free at 800-989-WILL. In my state we have a Commission on Aging that also has forms and assistance available. A similar agency probably exists in your state. Also, be careful in your selection of witnesses for these documents. For example, witnesses should not be related to you, nor should they be anyone who would inherit from you.

If you are into genealogy, the family medical tree will be fun for you. For the rest of us, it may be a little tedious. However, the medical history of a family can be useful, and potentially even life saving. Since some medical conditions are genetic or tend to occur more frequently in some families, knowledge of your family's history just may provide the key a physician needs in order to arrive at a diagnosis more quickly. If a physician knows you have a high potential risk for a disease, he can screen more closely and earlier. With today's medical advances, some diseases may be prevented or diagnosed early enough to cure. Some genetic diseases can now be revealed through simple tests to find out if one is a carrier. A negative test can provide peace of mind, for example, for a young couple wishing to have a baby. A positive test can, at least, advise you so you can weigh the situation in order to make an informed decision.

# DOCTORS' NUMBERS

Primary family doctor: _____ Phone: _____

Pediatrician: _____ Phone: _____

Dentist: _____ Phone: _____

Orthodontist: _____ Phone: _____

Other doctors

Allergist: _____ Phone: _____

Cardiologist: _____ Phone: _____

Ear/Nose/Throat: _____ Phone: _____

Internist: _____ Phone: _____

OB-GYN: _____ Phone: _____

Oncologist: _____ Phone: _____

Ophthalmologist: _____ Phone: _____

Optometrist: _____ Phone: _____

Orthopedist: _____ Phone: _____

Physical therapist: _____ Phone: _____

Psychiatrist/Therapist: _____ Phone: _____

Surgeon: _____ Phone: _____

_____ Phone: _____

_____ Phone: _____

_____ Phone: _____

_____ Phone: _____

# PERSONAL MEDICAL HISTORY

Name: _____ Birth date: _____

Blood type: _____ Social Security number: _____

Primary physician: _____ Phone: _____

Allergies to food, medicines, etc.: _____

_____

| Immunizations/Diseases | Year | Immunizations/Diseases | Year |
|---|---|---|---|
| Chicken pox | _____ | Bleeding problems | _____ |
| Diphtheria | _____ | Blood disease | _____ |
| Hepatitis A and B | _____ | Diabetes | _____ |
| HIB (or DPT + HIB) | _____ | Epilepsy | _____ |
| HIV + or AIDS | _____ | Healing problems | _____ |
| Measles | _____ | Heart disease | _____ |
| Mumps | _____ | High blood pressure | _____ |
| Pertussis | _____ | Kidney disorders | _____ |
| Polio | _____ | Respiratory | _____ |
| Rubella | _____ | Rheumatic fever | _____ |
| Tetanus | | Scarlet fever | _____ |
| _____ | _____ | _____ | _____ |
| _____ | _____ | _____ | _____ |

| Major illness/Surgery | Date | Doctor |
|---|---|---|

_____
_____
_____
_____
_____

## Medications/Prescriptions

| Medicine | Purpose | Doctor | Pharmacy and prescription # |
|---|---|---|---|

_____
_____
_____
_____
_____

Eyeglass prescription: _____

# PERSONAL MEDICAL HISTORY

Name: _____ Birth date: _____

Blood type: _____ Social Security number: _____

Primary physician: _____ Phone: _____

Allergies to food, medicines, etc.: _____

_____

| Immunizations/Diseases | Year | Immunizations/Diseases | Year |
|---|---|---|---|
| Chicken pox | _____ | Bleeding problems | _____ |
| Diphtheria | _____ | Blood disease | _____ |
| Hepatitis A and B | _____ | Diabetes | _____ |
| HIB (or DPT + HIB) | _____ | Epilepsy | _____ |
| HIV + or AIDS | _____ | Healing problems | _____ |
| Measles | _____ | Heart disease | _____ |
| Mumps | _____ | High blood pressure | _____ |
| Pertussis | _____ | Kidney disorders | _____ |
| Polio | _____ | Respiratory | _____ |
| Rubella | _____ | Rheumatic fever | _____ |
| Tetanus | _____ | Scarlet fever | _____ |
| _____ | _____ | _____ | _____ |
| _____ | _____ | _____ | _____ |

| Major illness/Surgery | Date | Doctor |
|---|---|---|
| | | |
| | | |
| | | |
| | | |
| | | |

Medications/Prescriptions

| Medicine | Purpose | Doctor | Pharmacy and prescription # |
|---|---|---|---|
| | | | |
| | | | |
| | | | |
| | | | |
| | | | |

Eyeglass prescription: _____

# PERSONAL MEDICAL HISTORY

Name: _____ Birth date: _____
Blood type: _____ Social Security number: _____
Primary physician: _____ Phone: _____
Allergies to food, medicines, etc.: _____
_____

| Immunizations/Diseases | Year | Immunizations/Diseases | Year |
|---|---|---|---|
| Chicken pox | _____ | Bleeding problems | _____ |
| Diphtheria | _____ | Blood disease | _____ |
| Hepatitis A and B | _____ | Diabetes | _____ |
| HIB (or DPT + HIB) | _____ | Epilepsy | _____ |
| HIV + or AIDS | _____ | Healing problems | _____ |
| Measles | _____ | Heart disease | _____ |
| Mumps | _____ | High blood pressure | _____ |
| Pertussis | _____ | Kidney disorders | _____ |
| Polio | _____ | Respiratory | _____ |
| Rubella | _____ | Rheumatic fever | _____ |
| Tetanus | _____ | Scarlet fever | _____ |
| _____ | _____ | _____ | _____ |
| _____ | _____ | _____ | _____ |

| Major illness/Surgery | Date | Doctor |
|---|---|---|
| | | |
| | | |
| | | |
| | | |
| | | |

Medications/Prescriptions

| Medicine | Purpose | Doctor | Pharmacy and prescription # |
|---|---|---|---|
| | | | |
| | | | |
| | | | |
| | | | |
| | | | |

Eyeglass prescription: _____

# PERSONAL MEDICAL HISTORY

Name: _____ Birth date: _____

Blood type: _____ Social Security number: _____

Primary physician: _____ Phone: _____

Allergies to food, medicines, etc.: _____

_____

| Immunizations/Diseases | Year | Immunizations/Diseases | Year |
|---|---|---|---|
| Chicken pox | _____ | Bleeding problems | _____ |
| Diphtheria | _____ | Blood disease | _____ |
| Hepatitis A and B | _____ | Diabetes | _____ |
| HIB (or DPT + HIB) | _____ | Epilepsy | _____ |
| HIV + or AIDS | _____ | Healing problems | _____ |
| Measles | _____ | Heart disease | _____ |
| Mumps | _____ | High blood pressure | _____ |
| Pertussis | _____ | Kidney disorders | _____ |
| Polio | _____ | Respiratory | _____ |
| Rubella | _____ | Rheumatic fever | _____ |
| Tetanus | _____ | Scarlet fever | _____ |
| _____ | _____ | _____ | _____ |
| _____ | _____ | _____ | _____ |

| Major illness/Surgery | Date | Doctor |
|---|---|---|
| | | |
| | | |
| | | |
| | | |
| | | |

Medications/Prescriptions

| Medicine | Purpose | Doctor | Pharmacy and prescription # |
|---|---|---|---|
| | | | |
| | | | |
| | | | |
| | | | |
| | | | |

Eyeglass prescription: _____

# MEDICAL FAMILY TREE

Name: _____ Born: _____ Died: _____

Relationship to me: _____

Occupation(s): _____

Diseases/Illnesses: _____

_____

_____

Cause of death: _____

Use tobacco? _____ How much? _____

Use alcohol? _____ How much? _____

Weight: Underweight _____ Normal _____ Overweight _____

Lifestyle (diet, exercise, etc.): _____

Special information: _____

Name: _____ Born: _____ Died: _____

Relationship to me: _____

Occupation(s): _____

Diseases/Illnesses: _____

_____

_____

Cause of death: _____

Use tobacco? _____ How much? _____

Use alcohol? _____ How much? _____

Weight: Underweight _____ Normal _____ Overweight _____

Lifestyle (diet, exercise, etc.): _____

Special information: _____

# MEDICAL FAMILY TREE

Name: _____ Born: _____ Died: _____

Relationship to me: _____

Occupation(s): _____

Diseases/Illnesses: _____

_____

_____

Cause of death: _____

Use tobacco? _____ How much? _____

Use alcohol? _____ How much? _____

Weight: Underweight _____ Normal _____ Overweight _____

Lifestyle (diet, exercise, etc.): _____

Special information: _____


Name: _____ Born: _____ Died: _____

Relationship to me: _____

Occupation(s): _____

Diseases/Illnesses: _____

_____

_____

Cause of death: _____

Use tobacco? _____ How much? _____

Use alcohol? _____ How much? _____

Weight: Underweight _____ Normal _____ Overweight _____

Lifestyle (diet, exercise, etc.): _____

Special information: _____

# MEDICAL FAMILY TREE

Name: _____ Born: _____ Died: _____

Relationship to me: _____

Occupation(s): _____

Diseases/Illnesses: _____

_____

_____

Cause of death: _____

Use tobacco? _____ How much? _____

Use alcohol? _____ How much? _____

Weight: Underweight _____ Normal _____ Overweight _____

Lifestyle (diet, exercise, etc.): _____

Special information: _____

Name: _____ Born: _____ Died: _____

Relationship to me: _____

Occupation(s): _____

Diseases/Illnesses: _____

_____

_____

Cause of death: _____

Use tobacco? _____ How much? _____

Use alcohol? _____ How much? _____

Weight: Underweight _____ Normal _____ Overweight _____

Lifestyle (diet, exercise, etc.): _____

Special information: _____

# MEDICAL FAMILY TREE

Name: _____ Born: _____ Died: _____

Relationship to me: _____

Occupation(s): _____

Diseases/Illnesses: _____

_____

_____

Cause of death: _____

Use tobacco? _____ How much? _____

Use alcohol? _____ How much? _____

Weight: Underweight _____ Normal _____ Overweight _____

Lifestyle (diet, exercise, etc.): _____

Special information: _____

Name: _____ Born: _____ Died: _____

Relationship to me: _____

Occupation(s): _____

Diseases/Illnesses: _____

_____

_____

Cause of death: _____

Use tobacco? _____ How much? _____

Use alcohol? _____ How much? _____

Weight: Underweight _____ Normal _____ Overweight _____

Lifestyle (diet, exercise, etc.): _____

Special information: _____

# CONSENT FORM FOR EMERGENCY MEDICAL TREATMENT AND/OR SURGERY FOR A MINOR

I, _____ of _____

(full address)

am the parent having legal custody or legal guardian of _____

_____, a minor, born _____, _____, with Social

Security number _____. I authorize any of the following adults,
individually,

_____, _____

_____, _____

to consent to any X-ray examination, anesthetic, medical or surgical diagnosis or treatment, and
hospital care, to be rendered to the minor under the general or special supervision and on the
advice of any physician or surgeon licensed to practice, and to consent to any X-ray examination,
anesthetic, dental or surgical diagnosis or treatment, and hospital care, to be rendered to the
minor by any dentist licensed to practice.

Dated _____     _____

(Signature)

Notarized by: _____

State of: _____

Commission expires: _____

Health insurance information:

Insurance company: _____

Address: _____

_____ Phone: _____

Policy number(s): _____

Name and Social Security number of primary insured: _____

# CONSENT FORM FOR EMERGENCY MEDICAL TREATMENT AND/OR SURGERY FOR A MINOR

I, _____ of _____
(full address)

am the parent having legal custody or legal guardian of _____
_____, a minor, born _____, _____, with Social
Security number _____. I authorize any of the following adults,
individually,

_____, _____

_____, _____

to consent to any X-ray examination, anesthetic, medical or surgical diagnosis or treatment, and
hospital care, to be rendered to the minor under the general or special supervision and on the
advice of any physician or surgeon licensed to practice, and to consent to any X-ray examination,
anesthetic, dental or surgical diagnosis or treatment, and hospital care, to be rendered to the
minor by any dentist licensed to practice.

Dated _____          _____
(Signature)

Notarized by: _____

    State of: _____

    Commission expires: _____

Health insurance information:

  Insurance company: _____

  Address: _____

  _____ Phone: _____

  Policy number(s): _____

  Name and Social Security number of primary insured: _____

# Consent Form for Emergency Medical Treatment and/or Surgery for a Minor

I, _____ of _____

(full address)

am the parent having legal custody or legal guardian of _____

_____, a minor, born _____, _____, with Social

Security number _____. I authorize any of the following adults,
individually,

_____, _____

_____, _____

to consent to any X-ray examination, anesthetic, medical or surgical diagnosis or treatment, and
hospital care, to be rendered to the minor under the general or special supervision and on the
advice of any physician or surgeon licensed to practice, and to consent to any X-ray examination,
anesthetic, dental or surgical diagnosis or treatment, and hospital care, to be rendered to the
minor by any dentist licensed to practice.

Dated _____          _____

(Signature)

Notarized by: _____

State of: _____

Commission expires: _____

Health insurance information:

Insurance company: _____

Address: _____

_____ Phone: _____

Policy number(s): _____

Name and Social Security number of primary insured: _____

# CONSENT FORM FOR EMERGENCY MEDICAL TREATMENT AND/OR SURGERY FOR A MINOR

I, _____ of _____
                                          (full address)

am the parent having legal custody or legal guardian of _____
_____, a minor, born _____, _____, with Social
Security number _____. I authorize any of the following adults,
individually,

_____, _____

_____, _____

to consent to any X-ray examination, anesthetic, medical or surgical diagnosis or treatment, and
hospital care, to be rendered to the minor under the general or special supervision and on the
advice of any physician or surgeon licensed to practice, and to consent to any X-ray examination,
anesthetic, dental or surgical diagnosis or treatment, and hospital care, to be rendered to the
minor by any dentist licensed to practice.

Dated _____        _____
                                                   (Signature)

Notarized by: _____

        State of: _____

        Commission expires: _____

Health insurance information:

  Insurance company: _____

  Address: _____

           _____ Phone: _____

  Policy number(s): _____

  Name and Social Security number of primary insured: _____

# Living Will

I, _____, willfully and voluntarily make known my desire that my dying shall not be artificially prolonged under the circumstances set forth below, and do hereby declare:

If at any time I should have a terminal condition and my attending physician has determined there is no reasonable medical expectation of recovery and which, as a medical probability, will result in my death, regardless of the use or discontinuance of medical treatment implemented for the purpose of sustaining life, or the life process, I direct that medical care be withheld or withdrawn, and that I be permitted to die naturally with only the administration of medications or the performance of any medical procedure deemed necessary to provide me with comfortable care or to alleviate pain.

## Artificially Provided Nourishment and Fluids

By checking the appropriate line below, I specifically:

_____ Authorize the withholding or withdrawal of artificially provided food, water, or other nourishment or fluids.

_____ *Do not* authorize the withholding or withdrawal of artificially provided food, water, or other nourishment or fluids.

## Organ Donor Certification

Notwithstanding my previous declaration relative to the withholding or withdrawal of life-prolonging procedures, if as indicated below I have expressed my desire to donate my organs and/or tissues for transplantation, or any of them as specifically designated herein, I do direct my attending physician, if I have been determined dead according to the laws of my state, to maintain me on artificial-support systems only for the period of time required to maintain the viability of and to remove such organs and/or tissues.

By checking the appropriate line below, I specifically:

_____ Desire to donate my organs and/or tissues for transplantation

_____ Desire to donate my _____
(Indicate specific organs and/or tissues for transplantation.)

_____ *Do not* desire to donate my organs or tissues for transplantation

In the absence of my ability to give directions regarding my medical care, it is my intention that this declaration shall be honored by my family and physician as the final expression of my legal right to refuse medical care and accept the consequences of such refusal.

The definitions of terms used herein shall be as set forth in the laws of my state regarding the right to natural death.

I understand the full import of this declaration, and I am emotionally and mentally competent to make this declaration.

In acknowledgment whereof, I do hereinafter affix my signature on this the _____ day of _____, 19_____.

_____
(Declarant)

We, the subscribing witnesses hereto, are personally acquainted with and subscribe our names hereto at the request of the declarant, an adult whom we believe to be of sound mind, fully aware of the action taken herein and its possible consequence.

We, the undersigned witnesses, further declare that we are not related to the declarant by blood or marriage; that we are not entitled to any portion of the estate of the declarant upon the declarant's decease under any will or codicil thereto presently existing or by operation of law then existing; that we are not the attending physician or a health facility in which the declarant is a patient; and that we are not persons who, at the present time, have a claim against any portion of the estate of the declarant upon the declarant's death.

_____
(Witness)

_____
(Witness)

State of: _____
County of: _____
Subscribed, sworn to, and acknowledged before me by _____, the declarant, and subscribed and sworn to before me by _____ and _____, witnesses, this _____ day of _____, 19_____.
My commission expires: _____   _____
(Notary Public)

# LIVING WILL

I, _____, willfully and voluntarily make known my desire that my dying shall not be artificially prolonged under the circumstances set forth below, and do hereby declare:

If at any time I should have a terminal condition and my attending physician has determined there is no reasonable medical expectation of recovery and which, as a medical probability, will result in my death, regardless of the use or discontinuance of medical treatment implemented for the purpose of sustaining life, or the life process, I direct that medical care be withheld or withdrawn, and that I be permitted to die naturally with only the administration of medications or the performance of any medical procedure deemed necessary to provide me with comfortable care or to alleviate pain.

## Artificially Provided Nourishment and Fluids

By checking the appropriate line below, I specifically:

_____ Authorize the withholding or withdrawal of artificially provided food, water, or other nourishment or fluids.

_____ *Do not* authorize the withholding or withdrawal of artificially provided food, water, or other nourishment or fluids.

## Organ Donor Certification

Notwithstanding my previous declaration relative to the withholding or withdrawal of life-prolonging procedures, if as indicated below I have expressed my desire to donate my organs and/or tissues for transplantation, or any of them as specifically designated herein, I do direct my attending physician, if I have been determined dead according to the laws of my state, to maintain me on artificial-support systems only for the period of time required to maintain the viability of and to remove such organs and/or tissues.

By checking the appropriate line below, I specifically:

_____ Desire to donate my organs and/or tissues for transplantation

_____ Desire to donate my _____
(Indicate specific organs and/or tissues for transplantation.)

_____ *Do not* desire to donate my organs or tissues for transplantation

In the absence of my ability to give directions regarding my medical care, it is my intention that this declaration shall be honored by my family and physician as the final expression of my legal right to refuse medical care and accept the consequences of such refusal.

The definitions of terms used herein shall be as set forth in the laws of my state regarding the right to natural death.

I understand the full import of this declaration, and I am emotionally and mentally competent to make this declaration.

In acknowledgment whereof, I do hereinafter affix my signature on this the _____ day of _____, 19_____.

_____
(Declarant)

We, the subscribing witnesses hereto, are personally acquainted with and subscribe our names hereto at the request of the declarant, an adult whom we believe to be of sound mind, fully aware of the action taken herein and its possible consequence.

We, the undersigned witnesses, further declare that we are not related to the declarant by blood or marriage; that we are not entitled to any portion of the estate of the declarant upon the declarant's decease under any will or codicil thereto presently existing or by operation of law then existing; that we are not the attending physician or a health facility in which the declarant is a patient; and that we are not persons who, at the present time, have a claim against any portion of the estate of the declarant upon the declarant's death.

_____
(Witness)

_____
(Witness)

State of: _____

County of: _____

Subscribed, sworn to, and acknowledged before me by _____, the declarant, and subscribed and sworn to before me by _____ and _____, witnesses, this _____ day of _____, 19_____.

My commission expires: _____    _____
(Notary Public)

# FINANCIAL RECORDS

Some people will need to complete every page of the financial section, while the rest will need only a few of the pages. The information in this section may be helpful when updating your financial statement, invaluable if you have lost your credit cards, or perhaps just a good reminder that you need to update your will. While you may feel some of this section is unnecessary to complete, put yourself in your executor's shoes trying to find all of the important information. The more information you can include, the better off you and your family will be in a time of crisis. Some pages may not be pertinent at this time. Leave them blank for now. Someday you may need them.

The pages on bank accounts, stocks, trusts, and so forth are fairly straightforward. Other assets of significant value should be noted. *Be sure to indicate where to find items whose locations are not immediately obvious.* Various members of my family remind me from time to time where certain items are hidden. I am very concerned the day will come when I must locate these items, and I will forget some. Receivables and liabilities are also important to have written down somewhere in an organized way.

If your wallet is stolen, do you know what credit cards you have? What are the credit card numbers? What numbers do you call to report the theft? A list summarizing your credit cards can streamline your work. I keep a file containing the documents that come with my credit cards in the event I need some address or other information. If you keep these documents filed alphabetically, when a replacement card arrives, you can easily remove the old document and insert the new.

Periodically, I take all of my cards out of my purse and put about eight at a time on the copier. This way I have an exact record of what is in my purse so I can be confident whom to contact in the event of a loss. In addition to credit cards, I include everything I carry including airline cards, telephone cards, library cards, and membership cards. I keep this copy in the same credit card file. For those who travel frequently, you may consider separating those cards you use at home from those you use while traveling. I have a separate case where I keep everything I use locally. When I travel, the case is "filed" with my credit card file. When I travel, I carry my wallet with my Master-Card, VISA, various car rental and airline cards, upgrade stickers, telephone cards, a couple of gas cards, business cards, my driver's license, health insurance card, Band-aids, safety pins, and even some cash! I even carry a card on which is written all of the family's Social Security numbers, driver's license numbers, and bank account numbers. I have used this countless times. As bad as all of this sounds, the wallet is amazingly slim, and I can survive in almost any circumstance anywhere in the world with it.

Do you know where your safe deposit box is? What about where the key is kept? Does your spouse know? For many a widow or widower, an already difficult time in their lives was made even more traumatic because a loved one had not kept them informed. An easy place to keep your key is in this book. For those who are worried someone else could use the key, remember the banks must identify you and have you sign in. Your safe deposit box is great for safe storage for everything from jewelry to stock certificates. I recommend keeping in the safe deposit box items such as birth certificates, marriage certificates, death certificates, military-discharge papers, a copy of your home inventory (a thorough video of your home at least), car titles, etc. I recommend that you do not keep your insurance papers or your cemetery deed there. If you keep your will in the box, be sure other valid copies are available elsewhere. Also, I do not recommend that you have anything there that you might need in an emergency. Since I have family living abroad, I do not keep our passports there. Remember, emergencies can happen on weekends when banks are closed. Also, in the event of a death, safe deposit boxes are sealed. If you are authorized to open the safe deposit box, you may enter the box in the presence of a bank officer, but you may only remove certain critical items such as a cemetery deed, a will, and insurance policies. You may need a will to prove you are authorized. Normally, the box must be inventoried before anything else may be taken. When your original documents are in the safe deposit box, copies placed in your *Essential Home Record Book* notebook can be helpful.

Be sure to list all liabilities carefully. Should anything happen to you, it is very important for your family or executor to know any and all liabilities. Also, if you are using the contents of this section to create or update a financial statement, you must report all liabilities.

The vehicle lease is something about which I want to warn you to be very careful and to be sure you have really done your homework before you sign the dotted line. Car dealers love leasing. This should be your first clue that you should be cautious. There are many excellent books available on leasing that will help consumers know exactly what their commitment and costs are.

Record the retirement benefits to which you are entitled. As we age, sometimes we become forgetful. By having everything written down, you (or someone in your family assisting you) can be sure nothing is overlooked. It may just be a good reminder that everyone should be sure retirement income will be sufficient. This provides an opportunity to review what is in place, and decide if any adjustments should be made.

While the durable power-of-attorney may never be needed, it is very important. Why? You say, "I can take care of myself, and my will takes care of my family when I am gone." Fine, but what happens if you are so ill or injured that you cannot take care of yourself, but you are still alive? Is anyone authorized to take care of your financial affairs? If you and your spouse name each other and travel together, you are still at risk. Please consult with your attorney. Review and update your will, your living will, and your power-of-attorney.

# BANK ACCOUNTS

For all accounts—Location of extra checks: _____

Location of current year's statements: _____

Bank: _____ Address: _____

Officer: _____ Phone: _____

Assistant: _____ Phone: _____

| Type | Account Number | Who Is Authorized | Checkbook Location |
|------|----------------|-------------------|--------------------|
| Checking | _____ | _____ | _____ |
| Checking | _____ | _____ | _____ |
| Savings | _____ | _____ | _____ |
| Savings | _____ | _____ | _____ |
| Money Mkt. | _____ | _____ | _____ |
| _____ | _____ | _____ | _____ |
| _____ | _____ | _____ | _____ |

Bank: _____ Address: _____

Officer: _____ Phone: _____

Assistant: _____ Phone: _____

| Type | Account Number | Who Is Authorized | Checkbook Location |
|------|----------------|-------------------|--------------------|
| Checking | _____ | _____ | _____ |
| Checking | _____ | _____ | _____ |
| Savings | _____ | _____ | _____ |
| Savings | _____ | _____ | _____ |
| Money Mkt. | _____ | _____ | _____ |
| _____ | _____ | _____ | _____ |
| _____ | _____ | _____ | _____ |

# BANK ACCOUNTS

For all accounts—Location of extra checks:_____

Location of current year's statements: _____

Bank: _____ Address: _____

Officer: _____ Phone: _____

Assistant: _____ Phone: _____

| Type | Account Number | Who Is Authorized | Checkbook Location |
|---|---|---|---|
| Checking | _____ | _____ | _____ |
| Checking | _____ | _____ | _____ |
| Savings | _____ | _____ | _____ |
| Savings | _____ | _____ | _____ |
| Money Mkt. | _____ | _____ | _____ |
| _____ | _____ | _____ | _____ |
| _____ | _____ | _____ | _____ |

Bank: _____ Address: _____

Officer: _____ Phone: _____

Assistant: _____ Phone: _____

| Type | Account Number | Who Is Authorized | Checkbook Location |
|---|---|---|---|
| Checking | _____ | _____ | _____ |
| Checking | _____ | _____ | _____ |
| Savings | _____ | _____ | _____ |
| Savings | _____ | _____ | _____ |
| Money Mkt. | _____ | _____ | _____ |
| _____ | _____ | _____ | _____ |
| _____ | _____ | _____ | _____ |

# CREDIT CARD ACCOUNTS

| Name of Card/ Company | Card # | Expiration Date | Authorized Users | Phone # If Lost or Stolen | Credit Limit | Rate |
|---|---|---|---|---|---|---|
| | | | | | | |
| | | | | | | |
| | | | | | | |
| | | | | | | |
| | | | | | | |
| | | | | | | |
| | | | | | | |
| | | | | | | |
| | | | | | | |
| | | | | | | |
| | | | | | | |
| | | | | | | |
| | | | | | | |
| | | | | | | |
| | | | | | | |
| | | | | | | |

If you have credit card insurance coverage—Name of company: _____ Phone: _____

# REAL ESTATE—OWNED

Location: _____

Titled to: _____

Primary home: _____ Additional home: _____ Leased to others: _____

Commercial property: _____ Use: _____

If leased, to whom: _____ Phone: _____

Terms of lease: _____

Security deposit: _____ Terms of refund: _____

Date purchased: _____ Purchase price: _____

Mortgage holder: _____ Officer: _____

Address: _____ Phone: _____

Terms of mortgage—Date of origin: _____ Amount: _____

Number of years: _____ Balloon?: _____ Interest rate: _____

Payment: _____ Due: _____ Loan #: _____

Paid by check: _____ Automatic debit: _____ Account #: _____

Property taxes—Amount: _____ Due: _____

Homeowners' association: Name: _____

Address: _____

| Board: Name | Title | Phone |
|---|---|---|
| _____ | _____ | _____ |
| _____ | _____ | _____ |
| _____ | _____ | _____ |
| _____ | _____ | _____ |

Assessments/Dues—Amount(s): _____ Due: _____

Location of appraisal, deed of trust, deed of trust note, loan
   documents, title policy, warranty deed, HUD settlement
   statement: _____

_____

Location of files/receipts relating to major improvements: _____

_____

If there is a shared storage area:
   Location: _____

   Storage lock combination or key location: _____

# REAL ESTATE—OWNED

Location: _____

Titled to: _____

Primary home: _____ Additional home: _____ Leased to others: _____

Commercial property: _____ Use: _____

If leased, to whom: _____ Phone: _____

Terms of lease: _____

Security deposit: _____ Terms of refund: _____

Date purchased: _____ Purchase price: _____

Mortgage holder: _____ Officer: _____

Address: _____ Phone: _____

Terms of mortgage—Date of origin: _____ Amount: _____

Number of years: _____ Balloon?: _____ Interest rate: _____

Payment: _____ Due: _____ Loan #: _____

Paid by check: _____ Automatic debit: _____ Account #: _____

Property taxes—Amount: _____ Due: _____

Homeowners' association: Name: _____

Address: _____

Board: Name                          Title                          Phone

_____          _____          _____

_____          _____          _____

_____          _____          _____

_____          _____          _____

Assessments/Dues—Amount(s): _____ Due: _____

Location of appraisal, deed of trust, deed of trust note, loan
   documents, title policy, warranty deed, HUD settlement
   statement: _____

_____

Location of files/receipts relating to major improvements: _____

_____

If there is a shared storage area:
   Location: _____

   Storage lock combination or key location: _____

# REAL ESTATE—LEASED

Location: _____

Titled to: _____

Primary home: _____ Additional home: _____

Commercial property: _____ Use: _____

Leased from: _____ Phone: _____

Security deposit: _____ Terms of refund: _____

Special requirements (e.g., no pets): _____

_____

Date first leased: _____ Current lease expires: _____

Lease holder: _____ Contact: _____

Address: _____ Phone: _____

Terms of lease—Date of origin: _____ Amount: _____

Number of Years: _____ Payment: _____ Due: _____

Paid by check: _____ Automatic debit: _____ Account #: ____

Lease holders' association—Name: _____

Address: _____

Board: <u>Name</u>                    <u>Title</u>                    <u>Phone</u>

_____     _____     _____

_____     _____     _____

_____     _____     _____

_____     _____     _____

Assessments/Dues—Amount(s): _____ Due: _____

Location of lease documents: _____

If there is a shared storage area:

  Location: _____

  Storage lock combination or key location: _____

Landlord: _____ Phone: _____

Manager/Super: _____ Phone: _____

# REAL ESTATE—LEASED

Location: _____

Titled to: _____

Primary home: _____ Additional home: _____

Commercial property: _____ Use: _____

Leased from: _____ Phone: _____

Security deposit: _____ Terms of refund: _____

Special requirements (e.g., no pets): _____

_____

Date first leased: _____ Current lease expires: _____

Lease holder: _____ Contact: _____

Address: _____ Phone: _____

Terms of lease—Date of origin: _____ Amount: _____

Number of Years: _____ Payment: _____ Due: _____

Paid by check: _____ Automatic debit: _____ Account #: _____

Lease holders' association—Name: _____

Address: _____

Board: <u>Name</u>                    <u>Title</u>                    <u>Phone</u>

_____          _____          _____

_____          _____          _____

_____          _____          _____

_____          _____          _____

Assessments/Dues—Amount(s): _____ Due: _____

Location of lease documents: _____

If there is a shared storage area:

Location: _____

Storage lock combination or key location: _____

Landlord: _____ Phone: _____

Manager/Super: _____ Phone: _____

# SAFE-DEPOSIT BOX

Bank: _____

Branch: _____ Box number: _____

Address: _____

Location of keys: _____

People authorized to enter: _____

_____

Contents: _____

_____

_____

_____

_____

_____

_____

_____

_____

_____

_____

_____

_____

_____

_____

_____

_____

_____

# SAFE-DEPOSIT BOX

Bank: _____

Branch: _____ Box number: _____

Address: _____

Location of keys: _____

People authorized to enter: _____

_____

Contents: _____

_____

_____

_____

_____

_____

_____

_____

_____

_____

_____

_____

_____

_____

_____

_____

_____

# STOCKS, BONDS, T-BILLS, AND OTHER FINANCIAL ASSETS

Firm: _____ Address: _____

Broker: _____ Phone: _____

| Account Name | Type of Account | Account # | Who Is Authorized |
|---|---|---|---|
| _____ | _____ | _____ | _____ |
| _____ | _____ | _____ | _____ |
| _____ | _____ | _____ | _____ |

Location of files: _____

Firm: _____ Address: _____

Broker: _____ Phone: _____

| Account Name | Type of Account | Account # | Who Is Authorized |
|---|---|---|---|
| _____ | _____ | _____ | _____ |
| _____ | _____ | _____ | _____ |
| _____ | _____ | _____ | _____ |

Location of files: _____

Firm: _____ Address: _____

Broker: _____ Phone: _____

| Account Name | Type of Account | Account # | Who Is Authorized |
|---|---|---|---|
| _____ | _____ | _____ | _____ |
| _____ | _____ | _____ | _____ |
| _____ | _____ | _____ | _____ |

Location of files: _____

# STOCKS, BONDS, T-BILLS, AND OTHER FINANCIAL ASSETS (CONTINUED)

Securities held by individual:

Name of security: _____

Owner: _____

Number of shares: _____ Initial price per share: _____

If applicable: Interest rate: _____ Maturity date: _____

Certificate number(s): _____

Location of certificate(s): _____

Other information: _____

Name of security: _____

Owner: _____

Number of shares: _____ Initial price per share: _____

If applicable: Interest rate: _____ Maturity date: _____

Certificate number(s): _____

Location of certificate(s): _____

Other information: _____

Name of security: _____

Owner: _____

Number of shares: _____ Initial price per share: _____

If applicable: Interest rate: _____ Maturity date: _____

Certificate number(s): _____

Location of certificate(s): _____

Other information: _____

# STOCKS, BONDS, T-BILLS, AND OTHER FINANCIAL ASSETS

Firm: _____ Address: _____

Broker: _____ Phone: _____

| Account Name | Type of Account | Account # | Who Is Authorized |
|---|---|---|---|
| _____ | _____ | _____ | _____ |
| _____ | _____ | _____ | _____ |
| _____ | _____ | _____ | _____ |

Location of files: _____

Firm: _____ Address: _____

Broker: _____ Phone: _____

| Account Name | Type of Account | Account # | Who Is Authorized |
|---|---|---|---|
| _____ | _____ | _____ | _____ |
| _____ | _____ | _____ | _____ |
| _____ | _____ | _____ | _____ |

Location of files: _____

Firm: _____ Address: _____

Broker: _____ Phone: _____

| Account Name | Type of Account | Account # | Who Is Authorized |
|---|---|---|---|
| _____ | _____ | _____ | _____ |
| _____ | _____ | _____ | _____ |
| _____ | _____ | _____ | _____ |

Location of files: _____

# STOCKS, BONDS, T-BILLS, AND OTHER FINANCIAL ASSETS (CONTINUED)

Securities held by individual:

Name of security: _____

Owner: _____

Number of shares: _____ Initial price per share: _____

If applicable: Interest rate: _____ Maturity date: _____

Certificate number(s): _____

Location of certificate(s): _____

Other information: _____

Name of security: _____

Owner: _____

Number of shares: _____ Initial price per share: _____

If applicable: Interest rate: _____ Maturity date: _____

Certificate number(s): _____

Location of certificate(s): _____

Other information: _____

Name of security: _____

Owner: _____

Number of shares: _____ Initial price per share: _____

If applicable: Interest rate: _____ Maturity date: _____

Certificate number(s): _____

Location of certificate(s): _____

Other information: _____

# OTHER INVESTMENTS

Financial institution: _____

Address: _____

Contact person: _____ Phone: _____

Name on account: _____

Person(s) authorized: _____

Type of account: _____ Account number: _____

Location of records: _____


Financial institution: _____

Address: _____

Contact person: _____ Phone: _____

Name on account: _____

Person(s) authorized: _____

Type of account: _____ Account number: _____

Location of records: _____


Financial institution: _____

Address: _____

Contact person: _____ Phone: _____

Name on account: _____

Person(s) authorized: _____

Type of account: _____ Account number: _____

Location of records: _____

# OTHER INVESTMENTS

Financial institution: _____

Address: _____

Contact person: _____ Phone: _____

Name on account: _____

Person(s) authorized: _____

Type of account: _____ Account number: _____

Location of records: _____


Financial institution: _____

Address: _____

Contact person: _____ Phone: _____

Name on account: _____

Person(s) authorized: _____

Type of account: _____ Account number: _____

Location of records: _____


Financial institution: _____

Address: _____

Contact person: _____ Phone: _____

Name on account: _____

Person(s) authorized: _____

Type of account: _____ Account number: _____

Location of records: _____

# OTHER ASSETS (ANTIQUES, ART, JEWELRY, ETC.)

Asset: _____

Ownership: _____

Location of asset: _____

Location of appraisal/Files regarding asset: _____

_____

Asset: _____

Ownership: _____

Location of asset: _____

Location of appraisal/Files regarding asset: _____

_____

Asset: _____

Ownership: _____

Location of asset: _____

Location of appraisal/Files regarding asset: _____

_____

Asset: _____

Ownership: _____

Location of asset: _____

Location of appraisal/Files regarding asset: _____

_____

# OTHER ASSETS (ANTIQUES, ART, JEWELRY, ETC.)

Asset: _____

Ownership: _____

Location of asset: _____

Location of appraisal/Files regarding asset: _____

_____


Asset: _____

Ownership: _____

Location of asset: _____

Location of appraisal/Files regarding asset: _____

_____


Asset: _____

Ownership: _____

Location of asset: _____

Location of appraisal/Files regarding asset: _____

_____


Asset: _____

Ownership: _____

Location of asset: _____

Location of appraisal/Files regarding asset: _____

_____

# VEHICLE RECORDS—OWNED

Make: _____ Model: _____ Year: _____

Vehicle ID #: _____ License #: _____

Registered owner: _____

Principal driver: _____

Security code: _____ Hidden key location: _____

Date purchased: _____ Purchased from: _____

Address: _____ Salesman: _____

Warranty coverage: _____

Title #: _____ Location of title: _____

State registration renewal date: _____

Financed by: _____

Address: _____ Phone: _____

Make: _____ Model: _____ Year: _____

Vehicle ID #: _____ License #: _____

Registered owner: _____

Principal driver: _____

Security code: _____ Hidden key location: _____

Date purchased: _____ Purchased from: _____

Address: _____ Salesman: _____

Warranty coverage: _____

Title #: _____ Location of title: _____

State registration renewal date: _____

Financed by: _____

Address: _____ Phone: _____

# VEHICLE RECORDS—OWNED

Make: _____ Model: _____ Year: _____

Vehicle ID #: _____ License #: _____

Registered owner: _____

Principal driver: _____

Security code: _____ Hidden key location: _____

Date purchased: _____ Purchased from: _____

Address: _____ Salesman: _____

Warranty coverage: _____

Title #: _____ Location of title: _____

State registration renewal date: _____

Financed by: _____

Address: _____ Phone: _____


Make: _____ Model: _____ Year: _____

Vehicle ID #: _____ License #: _____

Registered owner: _____

Principal driver: _____

Security code: _____ Hidden key location: _____

Date purchased: _____ Purchased from: _____

Address: _____ Salesman: _____

Warranty coverage: _____

Title #: _____ Location of title: _____

State registration renewal date: _____

Financed by: _____

Address: _____ Phone: _____

# VEHICLE RECORDS—LEASED

Make: _____ Model: _____ Year: _____

Vehicle ID #: _____ License #: _____

Leasee/Principal driver: _____

Security code: _____ Hidden key location: _____

Date leased: _____ Leased from: _____

Address: _____ Salesman: _____

Warranty coverage: _____

Title #: _____ Holder of title: _____

State registration renewal date: _____

Lease expiration date: _____

List of lease benefits such as emergency assistance: _____

_____


Make: _____ Model: _____ Year: _____

Vehicle ID #: _____ License #: _____

Leasee/Principal driver: _____

Security code: _____ Hidden key location: _____

Date leased: _____ Leased from: _____

Address: _____ Salesman: _____

Warranty coverage: _____

Title #: _____ Holder of title: _____

State registration renewal date: _____

Lease expiration date: _____

List of lease benefits such as emergency assistance: _____

_____

# BOAT RECORDS

Make: _____ Model: _____ Year: _____

Hull ID #: _____ Boat name: _____

U.S. Coast Guard certificate of documentation #: _____

State registration #: _____

Registered owner: _____

Motor serial #: _____ Trolling motor #: _____

Inboard/Outboard engine #: _____ Outdrive #: _____

Transom plate #: _____

Trailer serial #: _____ Trailer license #: _____

Lock combination: _____ Location of key: _____

Marina slip or dry-storage location: _____

Date purchased: _____ Purchased from: _____

Address: _____ Salesman: _____

Warranty coverage: _____

Financed by: _____ Officer: _____

Address: _____ Phone: _____

# BUSINESS OWNERSHIP INFORMATION

Name of business: _____

Address: _____

Phone: _____, _____ Fax: _____ Mobile: _____

Sole proprietor: _____ Partnership: _____ Sub S corp: _____ Corporation: _____

If partnership or corporation, others involved:

Name: _____ Phone: _____

Address: _____

Name: _____ Phone: _____

Address: _____

Name: _____ Phone: _____

Address: _____

Nature of business or product: _____

Location of accounts receivable: _____

Accounts payable: _____

Appointment calendar: _____

Client list: _____

Employee records: _____

Inventory: _____

Inventory on order: _____

Other liabilities: _____

Payroll records: _____

Tax records: _____

Other: _____

# BUSINESS OWNERSHIP INFORMATION (CONTINUED)

Location of bank records—Current: _____

Prior years: _____

Bank: _____ Branch: _____

Bank officer: _____ Phone: _____

Assistant: _____ Phone: _____

| Account # | Who Is Authorized | Checkbook Location |
|---|---|---|
| _____ | _____ | _____ |
| _____ | _____ | _____ |
| _____ | _____ | _____ |

Accountant: _____ Phone: _____

Attorney: _____ Phone: _____

Bookkeeper: _____ Phone: _____

Insurance: _____ Phone: _____

_____ Phone: _____

_____ Phone: _____

Key employees:

Name: _____ Position: _____

Address: _____ Phone: _____

Name: _____ Position: _____

Address: _____ Phone: _____

Name: _____ Position: _____

Address: _____ Phone: _____

# EXPENSE REPORT—BUSINESS

Make extra copies of these forms. Be sure to fill them out regularly and keep the completed forms with your tax documents.

Purpose of trip, entertainment: _____

Advances—Date: _____ Amount: _____

Date: _____ Amount: _____

| Date | Description of Expense | Air/Train | Auto/Taxi | Hotel | Meals | Other | Total |
|------|------------------------|-----------|-----------|-------|-------|-------|-------|
|      |                        |           |           |       |       |       |       |
|      |                        |           |           |       |       |       |       |
|      |                        |           |           |       |       |       |       |
|      |                        |           |           |       |       |       |       |
|      |                        |           |           |       |       |       |       |
|      |                        |           |           |       |       |       |       |
|      |                        |           |           |       |       |       |       |
|      |                        |           |           |       |       |       |       |
|      |                        |           |           |       |       |       |       |
|      |                        |           |           |       |       |       |       |

Totals: _____

Less advances: _____

Due company: _____ /emp: _____

Attach receipts

# EXPENSE REPORT—PERSONAL

Trip: _____ Beginning cash on hand: Date: _____ Amount: _____

| Date | Description of Expense | Air/Train | Auto/Taxi | Hotel | Meals | Other | Total |
|------|------------------------|-----------|-----------|-------|-------|-------|-------|
|      |                        |           |           |       |       |       |       |
|      |                        |           |           |       |       |       |       |
|      |                        |           |           |       |       |       |       |
|      |                        |           |           |       |       |       |       |
|      |                        |           |           |       |       |       |       |
|      |                        |           |           |       |       |       |       |
|      |                        |           |           |       |       |       |       |
|      |                        |           |           |       |       |       |       |
|      |                        |           |           |       |       |       |       |
|      |                        |           |           |       |       |       |       |
|      |                        |           |           |       |       |       |       |
| Totals: |                     |           |           |       |       |       |       |

Total charges: _____

Total cash spent: _____

Attach receipts

# CHARITABLE CONTRIBUTIONS

| Date | Check # | Organization | If Gift-in-Kind, Description | Check Amount | Acknowledgment Received |
|------|---------|--------------|----------------------------|--------------|------------------------|
|      |         |              |                            |              |                        |
|      |         |              |                            |              |                        |
|      |         |              |                            |              |                        |
|      |         |              |                            |              |                        |
|      |         |              |                            |              |                        |
|      |         |              |                            |              |                        |
|      |         |              |                            |              |                        |
|      |         |              |                            |              |                        |
|      |         |              |                            |              |                        |
|      |         |              |                            |              |                        |
|      |         |              |                            |              |                        |
|      |         |              |                            |              |                        |
|      |         |              |                            |              |                        |
|      |         |              |                            |              |                        |
|      |         |              |                            |              |                        |
|      |         |              |                            |              |                        |

# CHARITABLE CONTRIBUTIONS

| Date | Check # | Organization | If Gift-in-Kind, Description | Check Amount | Acknowl- edgment Received |
|------|---------|--------------|------------------------------|--------------|----------------------------|
|      |         |              |                              |              |                            |
|      |         |              |                              |              |                            |
|      |         |              |                              |              |                            |
|      |         |              |                              |              |                            |
|      |         |              |                              |              |                            |
|      |         |              |                              |              |                            |
|      |         |              |                              |              |                            |
|      |         |              |                              |              |                            |
|      |         |              |                              |              |                            |
|      |         |              |                              |              |                            |
|      |         |              |                              |              |                            |
|      |         |              |                              |              |                            |
|      |         |              |                              |              |                            |
|      |         |              |                              |              |                            |
|      |         |              |                              |              |                            |
|      |         |              |                              |              |                            |

# BUSINESS GIFTS

| Date | Recipient | Description of Goods | Value |
| --- | --- | --- | --- |
| ____ | _____ | _____ | ____ |
| ____ | _____ | _____ | ____ |
| ____ | _____ | _____ | ____ |
| ____ | _____ | _____ | ____ |
| ____ | _____ | _____ | ____ |
| ____ | _____ | _____ | ____ |
| ____ | _____ | _____ | ____ |
| ____ | _____ | _____ | ____ |
| ____ | _____ | _____ | ____ |
| ____ | _____ | _____ | ____ |
| ____ | _____ | _____ | ____ |
| ____ | _____ | _____ | ____ |
| ____ | _____ | _____ | ____ |
| ____ | _____ | _____ | ____ |
| ____ | _____ | _____ | ____ |
| ____ | _____ | _____ | ____ |
| ____ | _____ | _____ | ____ |
| ____ | _____ | _____ | ____ |
| ____ | _____ | _____ | ____ |

# BUSINESS GIFTS

| Date | Recipient | Description of Goods | Value |
|------|-----------|----------------------|-------|
| _____ | _____ | _____ | _____ |
| _____ | _____ | _____ | _____ |
| _____ | _____ | _____ | _____ |
| _____ | _____ | _____ | _____ |
| _____ | _____ | _____ | _____ |
| _____ | _____ | _____ | _____ |
| _____ | _____ | _____ | _____ |
| _____ | _____ | _____ | _____ |
| _____ | _____ | _____ | _____ |
| _____ | _____ | _____ | _____ |
| _____ | _____ | _____ | _____ |
| _____ | _____ | _____ | _____ |
| _____ | _____ | _____ | _____ |
| _____ | _____ | _____ | _____ |
| _____ | _____ | _____ | _____ |
| _____ | _____ | _____ | _____ |
| _____ | _____ | _____ | _____ |
| _____ | _____ | _____ | _____ |

# RECEIVABLES:
## ACCOUNTS, LEASES, LOANS, OR NOTES

Debtor: _____ Address: _____

Home phone: _____ Office: _____ Mobile/Fax: _____

Type of receivable: _____ Date: _____

Terms of agreement: _____

Location of agreement: _____

Collateral: _____ Co-signer: _____

Nearest kin/Contact: _____ Phone: _____

Address: _____


Debtor: _____ Address: _____

Home phone: _____ Office: _____ Mobile/Fax: _____

Type of receivable: _____ Date: _____

Terms of agreement: _____

Location of agreement: _____

Collateral: _____ Co-signer: _____

Nearest kin/Contact: _____ Phone: _____

Address: _____


Debtor: _____ Address: _____

Home phone: _____ Office: _____ Mobile/Fax: _____

Type of receivable: _____ Date: _____

Terms of agreement: _____

Location of agreement: _____

Collateral: _____ Co-signer: _____

Nearest kin/Contact: _____ Phone: _____

Address: _____

# RECEIVABLES:
# ACCOUNTS, LEASES, LOANS, OR NOTES

Debtor: _____ Address: _____

Home phone: _____ Office: _____ Mobile/Fax: _____

Type of receivable: _____ Date: _____

Terms of agreement: _____

Location of agreement: _____

Collateral: _____ Co-signer: _____

Nearest kin/Contact: _____ Phone: _____

Address: _____

Debtor: _____ Address: _____

Home phone: _____ Office: _____ Mobile/Fax: _____

Type of receivable: _____ Date: _____

Terms of agreement: _____

Location of agreement: _____

Collateral: _____ Co-signer: _____

Nearest kin/Contact: _____ Phone: _____

Address: _____

Debtor: _____ Address: _____

Home phone: _____ Office: _____ Mobile/Fax: _____

Type of receivable: _____ Date: _____

Terms of agreement: _____

Location of agreement: _____

Collateral: _____ Co-signer: _____

Nearest kin/Contact: _____ Phone: _____

Address: _____

# LIABILITIES
# (NON–REAL ESTATE)

Lender: _____ Officer: _____

Address: _____ Phone: _____

Maker of note: _____

Original loan amount: _____ Date of origin: _____

Rate: _____ Loan #: _____ Date of maturity: _____

Terms: _____ Due: _____

Location of loan agreement: _____

Collateral or co-maker: _____

Purpose: _____


Lender: _____ Officer: _____

Address: _____ Phone: _____

Maker of note: _____

Original loan amount: _____ Date of origin: _____

Rate: _____ Loan #: _____ Date of maturity: _____

Terms: _____ Due: _____

Location of loan agreement: _____

Collateral or co-maker: _____

Purpose: _____


Margin Account—Company: _____

Broker: _____ Phone: _____

Records filed: _____

# LIABILITIES
# (NON–REAL ESTATE)

Lender: _____ Officer: _____

Address: _____ Phone: _____

Original loan amount: _____ Date of origin: _____ Rate: _____

Loan #: _____ Terms: _____ Due: _____

Location of loan agreement: _____

Purpose: _____


Lender: _____ Officer: _____

Address: _____ Phone: _____

Original loan amount: _____ Date of origin: _____ Rate: _____

Loan #: _____ Terms: _____ Due: _____

Location of loan agreement: _____

Purpose: _____


Lender: _____ Officer: _____

Address: _____ Phone: _____

Original loan amount: _____ Date of origin: _____ Rate: _____

Loan #: _____ Terms: _____ Due: _____

Location of loan agreement: _____

Purpose: _____


Margin Account—Company: _____

Broker: _____ Phone: _____

Records filed: _____

# LIABILITIES—VEHICLE LEASE

Lease holder: _____

Lease payments made to: _____

    Address: _____ Phone: _____

    Amount: _____ Due: _____

Leasee/Principal driver: _____

Vehicle dealer: _____ Phone: _____

Date of origin: _____ Down payment: _____

Security deposit/Reconditioning reserve: _____ Refundable?: _____

Lease-end value: _____ Penalty for early return: _____

Monthly lease payment: _____ For: _____ months

Total of lease payments: _____ Total cost of lease: _____

Lease—Open-ended: _____ Close-ended: _____

Advance payment option: _____

Purchase option—Price: _____ Market value: _____

    If the market value is more than the purchase option price,

    can the difference be applied toward the next lease? _____

Mileage allowance: _____ Refund for unused mileage: _____

Mileage charge over allowance

    Cost per mile if assessed at end of lease: _____

    Cost per mile if assessed at beginning of lease: _____

Terms for excess wear and tear: _____

Lease liability if vehicle is wrecked or stolen: _____

Gap insurance if wrecked or stolen: _____

# LIABILITIES—VEHICLE LEASE

Lease holder: _____

Lease payments made to: _____

    Address: _____ Phone: _____

    Amount: _____ Due: _____

Leasee/Principal driver: _____

Vehicle dealer: _____ Phone: _____

Date of origin: _____ Down payment: _____

Security deposit/Reconditioning reserve: _____ Refundable?: _____

Lease-end value: _____ Penalty for early return: _____

Monthly lease payment: _____ For: _____ months

Total of lease payments: _____ Total cost of lease: _____

Lease—Open-ended: _____ Close-ended: _____

Advance payment option: _____

Purchase option—Price: _____ Market value: _____

    If the market value is more than the purchase option price,

    can the difference be applied toward the next lease? _____

Mileage allowance: _____ Refund for unused mileage: _____

Mileage charge over allowance

    Cost per mile if assessed at end of lease: _____

    Cost per mile if assessed at beginning of lease: _____

Terms for excess wear and tear: _____

Lease liability if vehicle is wrecked or stolen: _____

Gap insurance if wrecked or stolen: _____

# TRUST FUNDS

I have created a trust for the benefit of: _____

_____

Trust was established on: _____

Trustees are: _____

Financial institution handling trust: _____

Trust officer: _____ Phone: _____

Legal firm that drew trust: _____

Attorney: _____ Phone: _____

The trust agreement and/or pertinent records are located at: _____

_____


I have created a trust for the benefit of: _____

_____

Trust was established on: _____

Trustees are: _____

Financial institution handling trust: _____

Trust officer: _____ Phone: _____

Legal firm that drew trust: _____

Attorney: _____ Phone: _____

The trust agreement and/or pertinent records are located at: _____

_____

# TRUST FUNDS (CONTINUED)

I am the beneficiary under a trust established by: _____

The trust agreement and/or pertinent records are located at: _____

_____

The trustees are: _____


I am the beneficiary under a trust established by: _____

The trust agreement and/or pertinent records are located at: _____

_____

The trustees are: _____


At my death, my heirs are beneficiaries of trust funds created by: _____

_____

The trust agreement and/or pertinent records are located at: _____

_____

The trustees are: _____


At my death, my heirs are beneficiaries of trust funds created by: _____

_____

The trust agreement and/or pertinent records are located at: _____

_____

The trustees are: _____

# RETIREMENT INCOME

## Social Security Benefits

Ninety days before retirement contact the Social Security office for an application for retiree's monthly income. (A nonworking spouse may also be eligible.) To apply, you will need the following:

- Social Security numbers
- Birth certificate(s); death certificate, if one spouse deceased
- Marriage certificate
- Most recent two years of W-2 forms

Decide if you wish to receive a check or have direct deposit, and if so, to what financial institution, and to what account.

Thirty to forty-five days before you want to begin payments, contact your employer's Human Resources/Benefits representatives.

*Note:* Records on vested retirement benefits from former employers since 1976 may be available through the Social Security office. Be sure to inquire regarding this information.

## IRA/Keogh/401K

Primary beneficiary: _____

Secondary beneficiary: _____

Name of financial institution: _____

Address: _____ Branch: _____

Officer: _____ Phone: _____

IRA: _____ Keogh/401K: _____ Account #: _____

Date funds available: _____ Date disbursements must begin: _____

Location of records: _____

# RETIREMENT INCOME (CONTINUED)

Primary beneficiary: _____

Secondary beneficiary: _____

Name of financial institution: _____

Address: _____ Branch: _____

Officer: _____ Phone: _____

IRA: _____ Keogh/401K: _____ Account #: _____

Date funds available: _____ Date disbursements must begin: _____

Location of records: _____


Primary beneficiary: _____

Secondary beneficiary: _____

Name of financial institution: _____

Address: _____ Branch: _____

Officer: _____ Phone: _____

IRA: _____ Keogh/401K: _____ Account #: _____

Date funds available: _____ Date disbursements must begin: _____

Location of records: _____


Primary beneficiary: _____

Secondary beneficiary: _____

Name of financial institution: _____

Address: _____ Branch: _____

Officer: _____ Phone: _____

IRA: _____ Keogh/401K: _____ Account #: _____

Date funds available: _____ Date disbursements must begin: _____

Location of records: _____

# RETIREMENT INCOME (CONTINUED)

## Annuities

Name of insurance company: _____

Name of representative/agent: _____

Name of representative's company: _____

Address: _____ Phone: _____

Primary beneficiary: _____

Secondary beneficiary: _____

Type of annuity: Fixed _____ Variable _____ Combination _____

Date funds available: _____ Date disbursements must begin: _____

Payment/Settlement options:

Straight life—Terms: _____

Life annuity with period certain—Terms: _____

_____

Joint and survivor annuity—Terms: _____

_____

Payment amount: _____ When: _____

Payment by check: _____ Direct deposit: _____ To account #: _____

Financial institution: _____

Early withdrawal option? Yes _____ No _____ If yes, then:

How: _____

Penalty: _____

Tax sheltered: _____ Tax deferred: _____

Other information: _____

Location of records: _____

# RETIREMENT INCOME (CONTINUED)

## Pension Plans

Name of primary beneficiary: _____

Name of additional beneficiary(ies): _____

Name of employer providing pension: _____

Address: _____

Contact: _____ Phone: _____

Name of company administering fund: _____

Address: _____

Contact: _____ Phone: _____

Name of fund: _____ Account #: _____

Date available: _____

How are benefits determined? _____

_____

_____

How is pension paid? Check _____ Direct deposit _____ Other: _____

   If direct deposit, to account #: _____ In name of: _____

   _____ at _____ (financial institution)

Amount paid: _____

If there are changes in the amount paid:

   When do changes occur? _____

   What effects could/would cause change? _____

Payments are received: Monthly _____ Quarterly _____ Semiannually_____

   Annually _____ Other: _____

Location of documents: _____

# RETIREMENT INCOME (CONTINUED)

## Pension Plans

Name of primary beneficiary: _____

Name of additional beneficiary(ies): _____

Name of employer providing pension: _____

Address: _____

Contact: _____ Phone: _____

Name of company administering fund: _____

Address: _____

Contact: _____ Phone: _____

Name of fund: _____ Account #: _____

Date available: _____

How are benefits determined? _____

_____

_____

How is pension paid? Check _____ Direct deposit _____ Other: _____

   If direct deposit, to account #: _____ In name of: _____

   _____ at _____ (financial institution)

Amount paid: _____

If there are changes in the amount paid:

   When do changes occur? _____

   What effects could/would cause change? _____

Payments are received: Monthly _____ Quarterly _____ Semiannually_____

   Annually _____ Other: _____

Location of documents: _____

# DURABLE POWER-OF-ATTORNEY

State of: _____

County of: _____


I, _____ of _____

(address), _____ (city), _____

(county), _____ (state), appoint _____,

my _____ (spouse *or* parent *or* child *or* . . .), of _____

_____ (address), _____

(city), _____ (county), _____ (state),

my attorney-in-fact, in my name, place, and stead, and for my use and benefit: powers to act in my

behalf to do every act that I may legally do through an attorney-in-fact.

This durable power-of-attorney shall not be affected by any disability on my part, except as

provided by the statutes of _____ (state). The power conferred on

my attorney-in-fact by this instrument shall be exercisable from _____

(date), notwithstanding a later disability or incompetence shall have the same effect and inure to

the benefit of and bind me or my heirs, devisees, and personal representatives as if I were competent

and not disabled.

This durable power-of-attorney shall be nondelegable and shall be valid until such time

as I _____ (die *or* revoke this power *or* am judged incompetent).

Dated _____        _____

                                                            (Signature)


Witnesses _____

                  _____

# DURABLE POWER-OF-ATTORNEY

State of: _____

County of: _____

I, _____ of _____

(address), _____ (city), _____

(county),_____ (state), appoint _____,

my _____ (spouse *or* parent *or* child *or* . . .), of _____

_____ (address), _____

(city), _____ (county), _____ (state),

my attorney-in-fact, in my name, place, and stead, and for my use and benefit: powers to act in my

behalf to do every act that I may legally do through an attorney-in-fact.

This durable power-of-attorney shall not be affected by any disability on my part, except as

provided by the statutes of _____ (state). The power conferred on

my attorney-in-fact by this instrument shall be exercisable from _____

(date), notwithstanding a later disability or incompetence shall have the same effect and inure to

the benefit of and bind me or my heirs, devisees, and personal representatives as if I were competent

and not disabled.

This durable power-of-attorney shall be nondelegable and shall be valid until such time

as I _____ (die *or* revoke this power *or* am judged incompetent).

Dated _____       _____

(Signature)

Witnesses _____

_____

# INSURANCE RECORDS

For me, completing this section on insurance is more than a little boring, but when this information is needed, your record will be invaluable. So don't put it off. Pull out those policies and get started. While you are completing this section on insurance, it is an ideal time to take advantage of having everything before you and assess your coverage.

- Be sure you have all the various types of coverage you need. For example, have you considered long-term-care insurance? When you are younger and healthier, it will be less expensive. Perhaps you have sufficient assets and this is an unnecessary insurance. Each type of insurance should be evaluated in light of need and cost.
- Be sure the level of coverage is adequate, comfortable, and current. Evaluate what level of deductibles you have. Would you be comfortable increasing the level of your deductibles in order to reduce your premiums? How much life insurance do you need? Have your needs changed? Have you added a baby to the family that needs to go to college someday? Is your last child educated and out of the nest? Do you have replaceable-cost insurance where assets are replaced at full value and not at a depreciated value?
- Be sure all contingencies are covered. What do I mean? For example, this summer my husband and children decided we *needed* a personal watercraft. (To those of you not up on these things, you might know the term waverunner or jet ski.) The marine insurance company that covers our sailboat would not cover our youngest child for two more years. I had to find another company that would insure someone of any age.

After you have evaluated everything and completed the forms, *do not* just stash those policies in a heap in some drawer. I have put mine in a separate notebook with plastic pages holding the various policies so I can easily turn through and find whatever I need. At each renewal, dispose of the old policy and insert the new policy. Remember, once you are organized, it is simple to stay organized.

I promise, you will feel really good when you have completed all of this. And you will know you are really ready should a crisis or problem occur.

# INSURANCE SUMMARY

| Type of Insurance | Expiration Date | Premium | Last Date Reviewed |
|---|---|---|---|
| Disability | _____ | _____ | _____ |
| Health/Dental/Major Medical | _____ | _____ | _____ |
| | _____ | _____ | _____ |
| | _____ | _____ | _____ |
| | _____ | _____ | _____ |
| Life | _____ | _____ | _____ |
| | _____ | _____ | _____ |
| | _____ | _____ | _____ |
| | _____ | _____ | _____ |
| Long-term care | _____ | _____ | _____ |
| Property | _____ | _____ | _____ |
| | _____ | _____ | _____ |
| | _____ | _____ | _____ |
| | _____ | _____ | _____ |
| Umbrella | _____ | _____ | _____ |
| Vehicle/Boat | _____ | _____ | _____ |
| | _____ | _____ | _____ |
| | _____ | _____ | _____ |
| | _____ | _____ | _____ |
| Other | _____ | _____ | _____ |

# DISABILITY INSURANCE

Individual(s) insured: _____

Coverage: _____

Limits—Illness: _____ Accident: _____

Issue date: _____ Policy #: _____

Premium: _____ Due: _____ How paid: _____

Insuring company: _____

Agent's company: _____

Address: _____

Agent: _____ Phone: _____

Location of policy: _____

Other information: _____

_____


Individual(s) insured: _____

Coverage: _____

Limits—Illness: _____ Accident: _____

Issue date: _____ Policy #: _____

Premium: _____ Due: _____ How paid: _____

Insuring company: _____

Agent's company: _____

Address: _____

Agent: _____ Phone: _____

Location of policy: _____

Other information: _____

_____

# HEALTH / DENTAL / MAJOR MEDICAL INSURANCE

Individual(s) insured: _____

_____

Coverage—Health: _____ Dental: _____
Deductible—Health: _____ Dental: _____
Plan #—Health: _____ Dental: _____
Issue date: _____ Policy #: _____
Premium: _____ Due: _____ How paid: _____
Insuring company: _____
Agent's company: _____
Address: _____
Agent: _____ Phone: _____
Location of policy: _____
Other information: _____

_____

Individual(s) insured: _____

_____

Coverage—Health: _____ Dental: _____
Deductible—Health: _____ Dental: _____
Plan #—Health: _____ Dental: _____
Issue date: _____ Policy #: _____
Premium: _____ Due: _____ How paid: _____
Insuring company: _____
Agent's company: _____
Address: _____
Agent: _____ Phone: _____
Location of policy: _____
Other information: _____

_____

_____

# HEALTH/DENTAL/MAJOR MEDICAL INSURANCE

Individual(s) insured: _____

_____

Coverage—Health: _____ Dental: _____

Deductible—Health: _____ Dental: _____

Plan #—Health: _____ Dental: _____

Issue date: _____ Policy #: _____

Premium: _____ Due: _____ How paid: _____

Insuring company: _____

Agent's company: _____

Address: _____

Agent: _____ Phone: _____

Location of policy: _____

Other information: _____

_____


Individual(s) insured: _____

_____

Coverage—Health: _____ Dental: _____

Deductible—Health: _____ Dental: _____

Plan #—Health: _____ Dental: _____

Issue date: _____ Policy #: _____

Premium: _____ Due: _____ How paid: _____

Insuring company: _____

Agent's company: _____

Address: _____

Agent: _____ Phone: _____

Location of policy: _____

Other information: _____

_____

_____

# HEALTH/DENTAL/MAJOR MEDICAL INSURANCE

Individual(s) insured: _____

_____

Coverage—Health: _____ Dental: _____

Deductible—Health: _____ Dental: _____

Plan #—Health: _____ Dental: _____

Issue date: _____ Policy #: _____

Premium: _____ Due: _____ How paid: _____

Insuring company: _____

Agent's company: _____

Address: _____

Agent: _____ Phone: _____

Location of policy: _____

Other information: _____

_____

Individual(s) insured: _____

_____

Coverage—Health: _____ Dental: _____

Deductible—Health: _____ Dental: _____

Plan #—Health: _____ Dental: _____

Issue date: _____ Policy #: _____

Premium: _____ Due: _____ How paid: _____

Insuring company: _____

Agent's company: _____

Address: _____

Agent: _____ Phone: _____

Location of policy: _____

Other information: _____

_____

# Life Insurance

Insured: _____ Owner: _____

Beneficiary(ies): _____

Issue date: _____ Maturity date: _____ Policy #: _____

Face value: _____ Cash value: _____ Loan value: _____

Premium: _____ Due: _____ How paid: _____

Policy assigned: _____ To whom: _____

Insuring company: _____

Agent's company: _____

Agent: _____ Phone: _____

Location of policy: _____

Other information: _____

_____

Insured: _____ Owner: _____

Beneficiary(ies): _____

Issue date: _____ Maturity date: _____ Policy #: _____

Face value: _____ Cash value: _____ Loan value: _____

Premium: _____ Due: _____ How paid: _____

Policy assigned: _____ To whom: _____

Insuring company: _____

Agent's company: _____

Agent: _____ Phone: _____

Location of policy: _____

Other information: _____

_____

# LIFE INSURANCE

Insured: _____ Owner: _____

Beneficiary(ies): _____

Issue date: _____ Maturity date: _____ Policy #: _____

Face value: _____ Cash value: _____ Loan value: _____

Premium: _____ Due: _____ How paid: _____

Policy assigned: _____ To whom: _____

Insuring company: _____

Agent's company: _____

Agent: _____ Phone: _____

Location of policy: _____

Other information: _____

_____

Insured: _____ Owner: _____

Beneficiary(ies): _____

Issue date: _____ Maturity date: _____ Policy #: _____

Face value: _____ Cash value: _____ Loan value: _____

Premium: _____ Due: _____ How paid: _____

Policy assigned: _____ To whom: _____

Insuring company: _____

Agent's company: _____

Agent: _____ Phone: _____

Location of policy: _____

Other information: _____

# LIFE INSURANCE

Insured: _____ Owner: _____

Beneficiary(ies): _____

Issue date: _____ Maturity date: _____ Policy #: _____

Face value: _____ Cash value: _____ Loan value: _____

Premium: _____ Due: _____ How paid: _____

Policy assigned: _____ To whom: _____

Insuring company: _____

Agent's company: _____

Agent: _____ Phone: _____

Location of policy: _____

Other information: _____

_____

Insured: _____ Owner: _____

Beneficiary(ies): _____

Issue date: _____ Maturity date: _____ Policy #: _____

Face value: _____ Cash value: _____ Loan value: _____

Premium: _____ Due: _____ How paid: _____

Policy assigned: _____ To whom: _____

Insuring company: _____

Agent's company: _____

Agent: _____ Phone: _____

Location of policy: _____

Other information: _____

_____

# LIFE INSURANCE

Insured: _____ Owner: _____

Beneficiary(ies): _____

Issue date: _____ Maturity date: _____ Policy #: _____

Face value: _____ Cash value: _____ Loan value: _____

Premium: _____ Due: _____ How paid: _____

Policy assigned: _____ To whom: _____

Insuring company: _____

Agent's company: _____

Agent: _____ Phone: _____

Location of policy: _____

Other information: _____

_____

Insured: _____ Owner: _____

Beneficiary(ies): _____

Issue date: _____ Maturity date: _____ Policy #: _____

Face value: _____ Cash value: _____ Loan value: _____

Premium: _____ Due: _____ How paid: _____

Policy assigned: _____ To whom: _____

Insuring company: _____

Agent's company: _____

Agent: _____ Phone: _____

Location of policy: _____

Other information: _____

# LONG-TERM-CARE INSURANCE

Individual(s) insured: _____

Insuring company: _____

Agent's company: _____

Address: _____

Agent: _____ Phone: _____

Location of policy: _____

Length of coverage: _____

Terms of coverage: _____

Issue date: _____ Policy #: _____

Premium: _____ Due: _____ How paid: _____

Scheduled changes and details:

   In length of coverage: _____

   In terms of coverage: _____

   In premium: _____

Other information: _____

_____

_____

_____

_____

_____

# LONG-TERM-CARE INSURANCE

Individual(s) insured: _____

Insuring company: _____

Agent's company: _____

Address: _____

Agent: _____ Phone: _____

Location of policy: _____

Length of coverage: _____

Terms of coverage: _____

Issue date: _____ Policy #: _____

Premium: _____ Due: _____ How paid: _____

Scheduled changes and details:

   In length of coverage: _____

   In terms of coverage: _____

   In premium: _____

Other information: _____

_____

_____

_____

_____

_____

# PROPERTY INSURANCE

Property insured: _____

Coverage: _____ Deductible: _____

Issue date: _____ Renewal date: _____ Policy #: _____

Premium: _____ Due: _____ How paid: _____

Insuring company: _____

Agent's company: _____

Address: _____

Agent: _____ Phone: _____

Location of policy: _____

Other information: _____

_____

Property insured: _____

Coverage: _____ Deductible: _____

Issue date: _____ Renewal date: _____ Policy #: _____

Premium: _____ Due: _____ How paid: _____

Insuring company: _____

Agent's company: _____

Address: _____

Agent: _____ Phone: _____

Location of policy: _____

Other information: _____

_____

# PROPERTY INSURANCE

Property insured: _____

Coverage: _____ Deductible: _____

Issue date: _____ Renewal date: _____ Policy #: _____

Premium: _____ Due: _____ How paid: _____

Insuring company: _____

Agent's company: _____

Address: _____

Agent: _____ Phone: _____

Location of policy: _____

Other information: _____

_____

Property insured: _____

Coverage: _____ Deductible: _____

Issue date: _____ Renewal date: _____ Policy #: _____

Premium: _____ Due: _____ How paid: _____

Insuring company: _____

Agent's company: _____

Address: _____

Agent: _____ Phone: _____

Location of policy: _____

Other information: _____

_____

# Umbrella Insurance

Liability coverage: _____

_____

Issue date: _____ Policy #: _____

Premium: _____ Due: _____ How paid: _____

Insuring company: _____

Agent's company: _____

Address: _____

Agent: _____ Phone: _____

Location of policy: _____

Other information: _____

_____

Liability coverage: _____

_____

Issue date: _____ Policy #: _____

Premium: _____ Due: _____ How paid: _____

Insuring company: _____

Agent's company: _____

Address: _____

Agent: _____ Phone: _____

Location of policy: _____

Other information: _____

_____

# VEHICLE/BOAT INSURANCE

Licensed drivers covered                    License #

_____                    _____

_____                    _____

_____                    _____

_____                    _____


Vehicle/Boat insured: _____

Coverage: _____ Deductible: _____

Issue date: _____ Term: _____ Policy #: _____

Premium: _____ Due: _____ How paid: _____

Insuring company: _____

Agent's company: _____

Address: _____

Agent: _____ Phone: _____

Location of policy: _____

Other information: _____


Vehicle/Boat insured: _____

Coverage: _____ Deductible: _____

Issue date: _____ Term: _____ Policy #: _____

Premium: _____ Due: _____ How paid: _____

Insuring company: _____

Agent's company: _____

Address: _____

Agent: _____ Phone: _____

Location of policy: _____

Other information: _____

# VEHICLE/BOAT INSURANCE

Vehicle/Boat insured: _____

Coverage: _____ Deductible: _____

Issue date: _____ Term: _____ Policy #: _____

Premium: _____ Due: _____ How paid: _____

Insuring company: _____

Agent's company: _____

Address: _____

Agent: _____ Phone: _____

Location of policy: _____

Other information: _____


Vehicle/Boat insured: _____

Coverage: _____ Deductible: _____

Issue date: _____ Term: _____ Policy #: _____

Premium: _____ Due: _____ How paid: _____

Insuring company: _____

Agent's company: _____

Address: _____

Agent: _____ Phone: _____

Location of policy: _____

Other information: _____

# OTHER INSURANCE

_____ insured: _____

Coverage: _____ Deductible: _____

Issue date: _____ Renewal date: _____ Policy #: _____

Premium: _____ Due: _____ How paid: _____

Insuring company: _____

Agent's company: _____

Address: _____

Agent: _____ Phone: _____

Location of policy: _____

Other information: _____

_____

_____ insured: _____

Coverage: _____ Deductible: _____

Issue date: _____ Renewal date: _____ Policy #: _____

Premium: _____ Due: _____ How paid: _____

Insuring company: _____

Agent's company: _____

Address: _____

Agent: _____ Phone: _____

Location of policy: _____

Other information: _____

_____

# EXTENDED-FAMILY RECORDS

This section may seem unnecessary at first glance, but experience has taught me how important and helpful this information can be. I became aware of the inadequate amount of information I knew about my in-laws when my mother-in-law had a stroke. The hospital staff knew we had been called and were packing to come as soon as possible. My father-in-law was so upset that the staff became concerned about him, called us, and wanted to know the name of his doctor. We had no idea whom to contact, and even though I was hundreds of miles away I needed to have access to basic information about my in-laws. Realizing how much I needed to know (and after thirty years did not know), I used them as my guinea pigs while writing this book. As one who now has been a caregiver for an extended period of time, and the eventual executor, I am relieved to have so much information gathered and available.

During the next few weeks following my experience, both parents of a friend were in the hospital at the same time, and both had life-threatening illnesses. Like me, she suddenly needed to know all kinds of information. She did not know where they banked, where insurance information was, or whom to contact. She was very helpful in suggesting the kind of information to include in *The Essential Home Record Book* that she needed during her time of crisis—information that would have been helpful and made her situation much less stressful.

One difficult topic for all of us to consider is funerals. While it may not be on the top of the list of things we wish to discuss with our extended family, perhaps by using the excuse of completing the book, you can more easily approach the subject. It is *always* easier to discuss funerals when everyone is healthy. Usually, decisions made during less emotional times will be better and more thorough. When the time comes, I want to know what my loved one wished. Somehow, it is comforting to know you are following his or her wishes.

Also included are generic forms for a durable power-of-attorney and for a living will. Again, in order to have the most proper, legal, and current forms available, have each person consult his or her attorney. I encourage you to have one of each signed for *each* person for whom you might ever be responsible. Carefully consider whom to designate as a durable power-of-attorney, and under what circumstances or conditions. My uncle signed a durable power-of-attorney designating my mother, but his doctor and lawyer were to determine with him or for him when to turn matters over to her. This proved invaluable when he became bedridden during the last six months of his life. While he could have signed such a document from his bed, that is not always an option. What if an accident occurs and one is in a coma? Again, to plan ahead and take care of these details without such pressure makes decisions more rational, less emotional, and much less traumatic.

Living wills also need to be considered while all is well. I am speaking from experience. My grandmother has made very clear her feelings about heroic efforts or about the use of machines to sustain her life. To show you how close this topic is to real life, at this time I am writing while sitting in her hospital room. Thirty-six hours ago she was rushed to the hospital, and the doctor thought she may die at any moment. She is now napping, but we just had lunch together and had a wonderful visit discussing everything from family to international current events. She has quickly improved, and we plan to take her home tomorrow. Who knows what the next hour, week, or month will bring? But we are prepared because we have been willing to talk, and we have completed necessary documents. We have not had to consider painful topics during a difficult time; rather, we have been able to discuss positive and happy topics and enjoy whatever time we have.

# EMERGENCY NUMBERS

Name: _____

Home address: _____ Zip: _____

Home phone: _____, _____, _____

Directions from nearest major intersection:

_____

_____

_____

_____

Fire #: _____ Police #: _____

Ambulance #: _____ Pet emergency #:_____

Poison control #: _____ Alarm company #: _____

Hospital—Name: _____ Phone: _____

Neighbor: _____

Address: _____

Home #: _____ Office #: _____ Mobile #: _____

Neighbor: _____

Address: _____

Home #: _____ Office #: _____ Mobile #: _____

Dentist: _____ Phone: _____

Doctors:

Allergist: _____ Phone: _____

Cardiologist: _____ Phone: _____

Gerontologist: _____ Phone: _____

Gynecologist: _____ Phone: _____

Internist: _____ Phone: _____

Oncologist: _____ Phone: _____

Ophthalmologist: _____ Phone: _____

Optometrist: _____ Phone: _____

Orthopedist: _____ Phone: _____

Physical therapist: _____ Phone: _____

Urologist: _____ Phone: _____

_____ Phone: _____

_____ Phone: _____

_____ Phone: _____

Drugstore: _____ Phone: _____

Drugstore that will deliver: _____ Phone: _____

Other important numbers: _____ Phone: _____

_____ Phone: _____

_____ Phone: _____

_____ Phone: _____

_____ Phone: _____

_____ Phone: _____

_____ Phone: _____

# LOCATION OF IMPORTANT DOCUMENTS

Name: _____

Appointment calendar: _____

Birth certificate: _____

Car title/Registrations: _____

Cemetery deed: _____

Death certificate: _____

Divorce/Separation: _____

Financial records: Check statements—Current year: _____

Prior years: _____

Payables: _____

Receipts: _____

Receivables: _____

Other: _____

Income tax returns: _____

Insurance policies: _____

_____

_____

Investment files: _____

IRA/Keogh: _____

Loan/Mortgage agreements: _____

_____

Marriage certificate: _____

Medical receipts/Insurance payments: _____

Medical records: _____

Military discharge, etc.: _____

Passport: _____

Real estate documents: _____

_____

Safe deposit box: _____

Stock investment files: _____

Trust: _____

_____

Will: _____

_____

Other

_____

_____

_____

_____

_____

_____

_____

# MEDICAL HISTORY

Name: _____ Birth date: _____

Blood type: _____ Social Security number: _____

Primary physician: _____ Phone: _____

Allergies to food, medicines, etc.: _____

| Immunizations/Diseases | Year | Immunizations/Diseases | Year |
|---|---|---|---|
| Chicken pox | _____ | Bleeding problems | _____ |
| Diphtheria | _____ | Blood disease | _____ |
| Hepatitis A and B | _____ | Diabetes | _____ |
| HIB (or DPT + HIB) | _____ | Epilepsy | _____ |
| HIV + or AIDS | _____ | Healing problems | _____ |
| Measles | _____ | Heart disease | _____ |
| Mumps | _____ | High blood pressure | _____ |
| Pertussis | _____ | Kidney disorders | _____ |
| Polio | _____ | Respiratory | _____ |
| Rubella | _____ | Rheumatic fever | _____ |
| Tetanus | _____ | Scarlet fever | _____ |
| _____ | _____ | _____ | _____ |
| _____ | _____ | _____ | _____ |

| Major illness/Surgery | Date | Doctor |
|---|---|---|

_____

_____

_____

_____

_____

Medications/Prescriptions

| Medicine | Purpose | Doctor | Pharmacy and prescription # |
|---|---|---|---|

_____

_____

_____

_____

_____

Eyeglass prescription: _____

Dental information: _____

# MEDICAL HISTORY

Name: _____ Birth date: _____

Blood type: _____ Social Security number: _____

Primary physician: _____ Phone: _____

Allergies to food, medicines, etc.: _____

| Immunizations/Diseases | Year | Immunizations/Diseases | Year |
|---|---|---|---|
| Chicken pox | _____ | Bleeding problems | _____ |
| Diphtheria | _____ | Blood disease | _____ |
| Hepatitis A and B | _____ | Diabetes | _____ |
| HIB (or DPT + HIB) | _____ | Epilepsy | _____ |
| HIV + or AIDS | _____ | Healing problems | _____ |
| Measles | _____ | Heart disease | _____ |
| Mumps | _____ | High blood pressure | _____ |
| Pertussis | _____ | Kidney disorders | _____ |
| Polio | _____ | Respiratory | _____ |
| Rubella | _____ | Rheumatic fever | _____ |
| Tetanus | _____ | Scarlet fever | _____ |
| _____ | _____ | _____ | _____ |
| _____ | _____ | _____ | _____ |

| Major illness/Surgery | Date | Doctor |
|---|---|---|
| | | |
| | | |
| | | |
| | | |
| | | |

## Medications/Prescriptions

| Medicine | Purpose | Doctor | Pharmacy and prescription # |
|---|---|---|---|
| | | | |
| | | | |
| | | | |
| | | | |
| | | | |

Eyeglass prescription: _____

Dental information: _____

Copyright © 1997 Pamela K. Pfeffer

# MEDICAL HISTORY

Name: _____ Birth date: _____

Blood type: _____ Social Security number: _____

Primary physician: _____ Phone: _____

Allergies to food, medicines, etc.: _____

| Immunizations/Diseases | Year | Immunizations/Diseases | Year |
|---|---|---|---|
| Chicken pox | _____ | Bleeding problems | _____ |
| Diphtheria | _____ | Blood disease | _____ |
| Hepatitis A and B | _____ | Diabetes | _____ |
| HIB (or DPT + HIB) | _____ | Epilepsy | _____ |
| HIV + or AIDS | _____ | Healing problems | _____ |
| Measles | _____ | Heart disease | _____ |
| Mumps | _____ | High blood pressure | _____ |
| Pertussis | _____ | Kidney disorders | _____ |
| Polio | _____ | Respiratory | _____ |
| Rubella | _____ | Rheumatic fever | _____ |
| Tetanus | _____ | Scarlet fever | _____ |
| _____ | _____ | _____ | _____ |
| _____ | _____ | _____ | _____ |

| Major illness/Surgery | Date | Doctor |
|---|---|---|
| | | |
| | | |
| | | |
| | | |
| | | |

## Medications/Prescriptions

| Medicine | Purpose | Doctor | Pharmacy and prescription # |
|---|---|---|---|
| | | | |
| | | | |
| | | | |
| | | | |

Eyeglass prescription: _____

Dental information: _____

# MEDICAL HISTORY

Name: _____ Birth date: _____

Blood type: _____ Social Security number: _____

Primary physician: _____ Phone: _____

Allergies to food, medicines, etc.: _____

| Immunizations/Diseases | Year | Immunizations/Diseases | Year |
|---|---|---|---|
| Chicken pox | _____ | Bleeding problems | _____ |
| Diphtheria | _____ | Blood disease | _____ |
| Hepatitis A and B | _____ | Diabetes | _____ |
| HIB (or DPT + HIB) | _____ | Epilepsy | _____ |
| HIV + or AIDS | _____ | Healing problems | _____ |
| Measles | _____ | Heart disease | _____ |
| Mumps | _____ | High blood pressure | _____ |
| Pertussis | _____ | Kidney disorders | _____ |
| Polio | _____ | Respiratory | _____ |
| Rubella | _____ | Rheumatic fever | _____ |
| Tetanus | _____ | Scarlet fever | _____ |
| _____ | _____ | _____ | _____ |
| _____ | _____ | _____ | _____ |

| Major illness/Surgery | Date | Doctor |
|---|---|---|
| _____ | _____ | _____ |
| _____ | _____ | _____ |
| _____ | _____ | _____ |
| _____ | _____ | _____ |
| _____ | _____ | _____ |

## Medications/Prescriptions

| Medicine | Purpose | Doctor | Pharmacy and prescription # |
|---|---|---|---|
| _____ | _____ | _____ | _____ |
| _____ | _____ | _____ | _____ |
| _____ | _____ | _____ | _____ |
| _____ | _____ | _____ | _____ |

Eyeglass prescription: _____

Dental information: _____

# KEY ADVISERS AND CONTACTS

Name: _____

Accountant: _____ Phone: _____

  Address: _____

Attorney: _____ Phone: _____

  Address: _____

Attorney: _____ Phone: _____

  Address: _____

Bank: _____ Branch: _____

Banker: _____ Phone: _____

  Address: _____

Bank: _____

Banker: _____ Phone: _____

  Address: _____

Church: _____

Clergy: _____ Phone: _____

  Address: _____

Financial adviser: _____ Phone: _____

  Address: _____

Insurance agent

  Disability: _____ Phone: _____

    Address: _____

  Health: _____ Phone: _____

    Address: _____

# KEY ADVISERS AND CONTACTS (CONTINUED)

Life: _____ Phone: _____

    Address: _____

Real estate: _____ Phone: _____

    Address: _____

Vehicle: _____ Phone: _____

    Address: _____

Marine/Boat: _____ Phone: _____

    Address: _____

Stockbroker company: _____

Stockbroker: _____ Phone: _____

    Address: _____

Stockbroker company: _____

Stockbroker: _____ Phone: _____

    Address: _____

Trust company: _____

Trust officer: _____

    Address: _____

_____ Phone: _____

    Address: _____

_____ Phone: _____

    Address: _____

_____ Phone: _____

# DISTRIBUTION OF PROPERTY

In addition to my will and any codicil that may exist, I wish to designate that the following items be given to the indicated individual:

Pet(s): _____ Individual: _____

Item: _____ Individual: _____

Item: _____ Individual: _____

Item: _____ Individual: _____

Item: _____ Individual: _____

Item: _____ Individual: _____

Item: _____ Individual: _____

Item: _____ Individual: _____

Item: _____ Individual: _____

Item: _____ Individual: _____

Item: _____ Individual: _____

Item: _____ Individual: _____

Item: _____ Individual: _____

Item: _____ Individual: _____

Item: _____ Individual: _____

Item: _____ Individual: _____

Item: _____ Individual: _____

Item: _____ Individual: _____

Item: _____ Individual: _____

Item: _____ Individual: _____

Item: _____ Individual: _____

Item: _____ Individual: _____

Item: _____ Individual: _____

Date: _____ _____
(Signature)

# DISTRIBUTION OF PROPERTY

In addition to my will and any codicil that may exist, I wish to designate that the following items be given to the indicated individual:

Pet(s): _____  Individual: _____

Item: _____  Individual: _____

Item: _____  Individual: _____

Item: _____  Individual: _____

Item: _____  Individual: _____

Item: _____  Individual: _____

Item: _____  Individual: _____

Item: _____  Individual: _____

Item: _____  Individual: _____

Item: _____  Individual: _____

Item: _____  Individual: _____

Item: _____  Individual: _____

Item: _____  Individual: _____

Item: _____  Individual: _____

Item: _____  Individual: _____

Item: _____  Individual: _____

Item: _____  Individual: _____

Item: _____  Individual: _____

Item: _____  Individual: _____

Item: _____  Individual: _____

Item: _____  Individual: _____

Item: _____  Individual: _____

Date: _____  _____

(Signature)

# LIVING WILL

I, _____, willfully and voluntarily make known my desire that my dying shall not be artificially prolonged under the circumstances set forth below, and do hereby declare:

If at any time I should have a terminal condition and my attending physician has determined there is no reasonable medical expectation of recovery and which, as a medical probability, will result in my death, regardless of the use or discontinuance of medical treatment implemented for the purpose of sustaining life, or the life process, I direct that medical care be withheld or withdrawn, and that I be permitted to die naturally with only the administration of medications or the performance of any medical procedure deemed necessary to provide me with comfortable care or to alleviate pain.

## Artificially Provided Nourishment and Fluids

By checking the appropriate line below, I specifically:

_____ Authorize the withholding or withdrawal of artificially provided food, water, or other nourishment or fluids.

_____ *Do not* authorize the withholding or withdrawal of artificially provided food, water, or other nourishment or fluids.

## Organ Donor Certification

Notwithstanding my previous declaration relative to the withholding or withdrawal of life-prolonging procedures, if as indicated below I have expressed my desire to donate my organs and/or tissues for transplantation, or any of them as specifically designated herein, I do direct my attending physician, if I have been determined dead according to the laws of my state, to maintain me on artificial-support systems only for the period of time required to maintain the viability of and to remove such organs and/or tissues.

By checking the appropriate line below, I specifically:

_____ Desire to donate my organs and/or tissues for transplantation
_____ Desire to donate my _____
(Indicate specific organs and/or tissues for transplantation.)
_____ *Do not* desire to donate my organs or tissues for transplantation

In the absence of my ability to give directions regarding my medical care, it is my intention that this declaration shall be honored by my family and physician as the final expression of my legal right to refuse medical care and accept the consequences of such refusal.

The definitions of terms used herein shall be as set forth in the laws of my state regarding the right to natural death.

I understand the full import of this declaration, and I am emotionally and mentally competent to make this declaration.

In acknowledgment whereof, I do hereinafter affix my signature on this the _____ day of _____, 19_____.

_____
(Declarant)

We, the subscribing witnesses hereto, are personally acquainted with and subscribe our names hereto at the request of the declarant, an adult whom we believe to be of sound mind, fully aware of the action taken herein and its possible consequence.

We, the undersigned witnesses, further declare that we are not related to the declarant by blood or marriage; that we are not entitled to any portion of the estate of the declarant upon the declarant's decease under any will or codicil thereto presently existing or by operation of law then existing; that we are not the attending physician or a health facility in which the declarant is a patient; and that we are not persons who, at the present time, have a claim against any portion of the estate of the declarant upon the declarant's death.

_____
(Witness)

_____
(Witness)

State of: _____
County of: _____

Subscribed, sworn to, and acknowledged before me by _____, the declarant, and subscribed and sworn to before me by _____ and _____, witnesses, this _____ day of _____, 19_____.
My commission expires: _____    _____
(Notary Public)

# DURABLE POWER-OF-ATTORNEY

State of: _____

County of: _____

I, _____ of _____
(address), _____ (city), _____
(county), _____ (state), appoint _____,
my _____ (spouse *or* parent *or* child *or* . . .), of _____
_____ (address), _____
(city), _____ (county), _____ (state),
my attorney-in-fact, in my name, place, and stead, and for my use and benefit: powers to act in my
behalf to do every act that I may legally do through an attorney-in-fact.

This durable power-of-attorney shall not be affected by any disability on my part, except as
provided by the statutes of _____ (state). The power conferred on
my attorney-in-fact by this instrument shall be exercisable from _____
(date), notwithstanding a later disability or incompetence shall have the same effect and inure to
the benefit of and bind me or my heirs, devisees, and personal representatives as if I were competent
and not disabled.

This durable power-of-attorney shall be nondelegable and shall be valid until such time
as I _____ (die *or* revoke this power *or* am judged incompetent).

Dated _____     _____

(Signature)

Witnesses _____

_____

# INDEX